35 by 35

A Runner's Quest

by

Taryn Spates

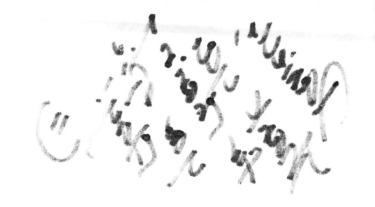

For my grandmother, Dorothy Norris

Table of Contents

Introduction

They can go ahead; it's fine. I'll catch up on the flat section just before the hill, then power past them with a few short, explosive bursts of my newfound speedy cadence — I hope. My legs are moving like I'm wearing watermelons for shoes. I should be feeling light and bouncy, but I am plodding along like a tired six-year-old at the end of a long day at Disneyland. I am not the seasoned marathon runner I have transformed into over the last fourteen years. A stranger has possessed my long legs and deep lungs, one who hates running. I love running. I love running marathons: the pain, the suffering, the incessant beat-down of morale that is consistent with every step up and down every hill, over every mile, in every race. Today it hurts.

Taryn Spates

Marathon #1 – San Diego Rock 'n Roll Marathon, 2001

Becoming A Grown Up

One of my best friends and former college roommate, Annie, asked me recently what made me start running marathons. She did not remember me being much of a runner at all in college. I was a bit taken aback by that question, because I have always considered myself a runner, but then I remembered my alcohol-infused frame of mind in college. Even though I did run, and worked out at the gym, I was far from the runner I was in high school, and light years away from the runner I would become. Still, to answer to Annie's question, I started running marathons because of my friend Hillary.

Hillary was another one of our roommates, and was a strong and consistent runner all throughout high school and college. She would run at least one hour every day no matter what. If it was snowing, if she was hung over, if she was cramming for an exam—it didn't matter. She ran every single day. That said, stepping up to the marathon was a big deal even for her. She never missed her needful long runs, or all of

3

the ones in between, and was ready to roll on race day.

It was cold and drizzly on race morning, but the leaves were blazing bright orange and danced across the Denver streets as all of my roommates piled out of our car partially asleep and still slightly drunk from the night before. We saw Hillary run past us screaming with glee, looking flushed and sweaty, but the happiest I had ever seen her. Suddenly, something clicked inside me. The rest of the morning was a bit foggy as I was battling a beast of a hangover, but watching and cheering for Hillary as she ran toward the finish line, smiling wide even though she was drenched from the rain, I vowed to run a marathon one day, too. *Thanks, Hill.*

I ran my first marathon on June 3, 2001. About a week before the race, I was dressed in my *Titanica* costume putting on a spectacle for many friends (and possibly a few random strangers off the street) as my roommates and I hosted another evening of G.L.O.W. (Gorgeous Ladies of Wrestling). If you are a child of the '80s you know exactly what this is, and I am proud to say that we represented loud and proud every time we suited up and took it to the living room floor.

My wrestler name was *Titanica* because I had an obsession with the movie *Titanic* during my freshman year in college; I saw it nine times in the theater. Yep, I was *that* girl. I even had a signature tag line that I bellowed to my opponents just before I body-slammed them into submission, "Your heart won't go on!" (*Thank you, Celine Dion.*)

My long red hair whipped from side to side while my large 5'10.5" frame overpowered each and every opponent I faced. It was a hysterical booze-infused night of fun. I had just graduated from the University of Colorado at Boulder about three weeks prior and was knee-deep in my post-graduate identity crisis of still living like a college student while only weeks away from moving back home to Los Angeles to start my career in the film industry. Plus, I was training for the Rock 'N Roll Marathon in San Diego.

I was nervous about the marathon, and life, for many reasons, mostly a fear of the unknown. My longest training run was nineteen miles, which was still seven miles shorter than the 26.2 I would be running on race day. I chose to take the "ignorance is bliss" approach; hence the previous weekend's drunken party time with my friends.

However, a funny thing happened on the way to the starting line. After my mom and stepdad, Kent, dropped me off a couple blocks away from the crowds, I hopped out of their Jeep and instantly felt a magnetic force pulling me toward the starting line. There I found my tribe. Runners stretching in the grass, fidgeting in the bathroom line, clapping and pumping each other up in the starting line corrals—I felt connected to all of them, and proud to be among them.

After the gun went off, and the miles started ticking away, I never thought that I couldn't do it; I just couldn't believe that I was *actually* running a marathon. At about mile seven, I hooked up with a seasoned female runner who was running a comfortable pace. We chatted briefly, she was nice, but I ditched her when she said, "At this pace we should finish in about five hours." Yeah, no thank you. I sped up and disappeared into the crowd without an explanation to my new not-so-speedy friend. Brutal, but I was on a mission to finish under 4:45.

The race took place in San Diego, California, which is home to one of the largest Marine bases in the country, Camp Pendleton. The most powerful image I remember from that day was of a buff, middle-aged Marine screaming at me while I ran past him, "Pain is weakness leaving your body!" I was both scared, and honored to be in his presence. Then a wave of shame washed over me as I realized that I was merely running a marathon that day, and felt exhausted, while he had committed his life to keeping me safe and protected, a true sacrifice. I promised myself in that moment that I would never allow myself to succumb to fatigue or pity. Instead, I would use it as fuel to push me harder through the dark moments. I owed him that much.

I veered off into "lonely town" at the halfway mark, mile 13.1. The course narrowed to a two-lane bike path, both the runners and spectators had thinned, and I was forced to have a real conversation with myself. There were no trees in sight, just hard cement pounding against my feet, and cool sweat dripping from my ponytail. I wasn't tired, but overwhelmed with sadness, because the single goal that I had been training for over the last six months was halfway over. I realized that I needed to drink it all in, because it would be over soon, along with so much else: college, living with my best friends, and living in Colorado. But in that moment, running on exhausted, tingly legs, I felt ready to handle every mile up ahead.

At about mile twenty-two, I heard frantic shouting from a distance. It was my brother Peter running out of Carl's Jr., chasing me down with a plastic order number in his hand. He cheered me on, and yelled that my pace was faster than he had thought (hence his assumption he had enough time to eat), but he promised to meet me at the finish line. This was not the first time that Peter had come in clutch for cheering me on to a spectacular finish; it was just another in a long line of big-brother heroics he had been displaying for most of my life. I was thrilled that he had made the commitment to support me for my first marathon, and having run side-by-side with him for those few paces made my day.

The last half-mile of the course looped around an expansive Marine base close to the airport, but I could not see the finish line through my sunscreen-drenched eyeballs. Then I turned left under a bridge and made one final sharp right turn toward the roaring crowds ahead. As I chased down those last few steps of the race, I felt super-human. I finished way under my goal in 4:24. Finally, I was awake and ready to grow up.

Peter running alongside me in the Rock 'n Roll Marathon

Marathon #2 – The Los Angeles Marathon, 2003

Welcome To The Real World

I graduated with a Bachelor's degree in Film Studies on May 11, 2001. I had wanted to be a filmmaker since I was ten years old, and now I had the education to support my dream. It may not come as a shock that it took some time to get my career up and off the ground in the misunderstood and elusive world of film and television production. Therefore, out of necessity, a month or so after my marathon I moved home to live with my dad and stepmother, Sally, in gorgeous Palos Verdes, California.

My dad is a successful businessman, and I think it is safe to assume that he had no idea how or why I was going to work in production. The way the accounting is structured in the film business is completely baffling; however, even though he had no idea how it all worked, or how he could really help me find work, he was supportive.

As fate would have it, my career soon took off after a chance encounter Sally had with a young couple on their honeymoon while on a cruise in Italy. The groom's name was

Anthony, and he was an actor/writer/producer who hit it off with Sally one afternoon on the pool deck. She approached him specifically to find me work when she saw him reading a Hollywood trade magazine. A few drinks and countless laughs later, he told her he would call me when they arrived home in Los Angeles to help me find production work. Mind you, this was all said in the middle of the Mediterranean, but Anthony kept his word, and actually called me. A few days after they arrived back in L.A., and after I had an unfortunate getting-lost-on-the-streets-of-Hollywood incident, Anthony and I finally met, and he quickly hooked me up with my first job. I was hired as a production assistant on a visual effects miniature shoot for a film called *Coronado*. Working on the movie was the toughest and most rewarding thirteen weeks of my life. I cemented a wonderful friendship with Anthony, memorized by heart the streets of Los Angeles, and brought home my very first paycheck.

After nine months that were long for all three of us, I finally moved out my parents' house and into my very own studio apartment in Venice, California. I thought it was the smallest and coolest apartment on the West Coast. There was minimal street parking, which meant I rarely had visitors, but I could walk to the beach to run along it day or night, and I was able to buy funky cheap sunglasses on the boardwalk every few weeks. It was perfect.

I had been working consistently as a production assistant, sufficiently surviving on my own, and loving every minute of my hectic life. However, in the beginning of November 2002, the television show that I had been working on for the past five months was canceled. While moping around during my last days on the show, I was flooded with the urge to run another marathon. After spending many, many hours over many days and nights in downtown Los Angeles where our stage was located, I decided I wanted to run the Los Angeles Marathon.

My TV show (*Haunted*) ended in early December 2002, and the marathon was slated for March 2, 2003, so I had about twelve weeks to whip myself back into marathon shape after not racing at all in 2002. Fortunately, I was not unemployed for long. I had another grueling twelve-plus-hours-a-day job lined up by early January, which meant, "Yay I can eat, but yikes, when am I going to train?" I will tell you when: before work, 6 to 8 a.m., and after work, 8 to 10 p.m. Night after night, from January to March, I ran loops around tract-home neighborhoods in Santa Clarita, California where the stage was located for my job. I sometimes ran in the rain, and always ran on exhausted legs, but none of that mattered because I had to train properly for the marathon. That being said, I still didn't know what I was doing.

I knew I had to run consistently throughout the week, and include a long run on the weekends, but I was not completely confident of my fitness level the night before the race. In fact, I worked the whole Saturday before the race on a friend's independent movie shoot. I gobbled up a few peanut-butter-and-jelly sandwiches throughout the day, and tried to drink a lot of water, but besides being sent home early to rest, I had no idea if what I was doing was going to help at all during the race.

The morning of the marathon was "L.A. sunny" but cold. I was decked out in my white on white sweat-wicking gear, the same outfit I had worn for the San Diego marathon, and blasted Eminem in my car during the nervous drive on the 10 freeway from Venice to downtown Los Angeles. As I walked from my car toward the starting line, I felt the ease of "my calling" calm my nerves; I was right where I was meant to be, on the starting line of another marathon. This time around, I was fueled by blood, sweat and tears that I had shed all over Los Angeles in my first full year of a working in production.

As the final minutes ticked by before the start, I stretched, and walked among the crowd of over 20,000 runners. The scent of sunscreen and fear flooded my nostrils. Suddenly, my heart skipped a beat. I saw her — my hero of all heroes — sitting among the dignitaries at the starting line: Jackie Joyner-Kersee.

I had been a hurdler and both a long and high jumper in high school during the mid-nineties when Jackie Joyner-Kersee was at her peak. I even had a poster of her on my bedroom wall when I was growing up, so to see her in real life mere steps away from me was beyond thrilling. It was a dream come true. As I stared in her direction, I swear she caught my gaze, and smiled. She may have been at looking at any of the other thousands of runners, but I felt her energy, and it gave me the confidence I needed just as the gun went off.

The present-day marathon course is a magnificent tour of Los Angeles. It is a "point to point" course starting at Dodger Stadium, and ending just above the ocean in Santa Monica. On the other hand, in 2003, the course was a meandering path

12

through South Central and the east side of Beverly Hills, highlighting the polarizing population of Los Angeles. Nevertheless, both demographics had two things in common during the marathon: they either loved it, and screamed and cheered their heads off as we ran past their homes, or they cursed us all as they waited in even longer than normal traffic due to the road closures. I was sympathetic to both corners of the ring, and was just happy to be yelled at one way or another; both were motivating.

The first seven miles I did not pay attention to my pace because I just wanted to finish under my previous time of 4:24. I wanted to be smart, and not bonk and blow my race by going out too hard, too quickly. After I passed mile fifteen, the road leveled out and was flat for the next five miles as we cruised through the Miracle Mile neighborhood, a historical area where museums and entertainment buildings loomed high in the sky above us. This part of the course was merciful because the tall buildings lent a healthy dose of shade to all of us hot and tired runners below. Moreover, there was tremendous crowd support, and a needful aid station with enthusiastic volunteers. One volunteer ran backwards, making me chase him for an energy gel. He may have thought he was being motivating, but I was simply annoyed. Nevertheless, I was passing people and feeling good.

Once we turned east onto Olympic Boulevard at mile twenty-two, the sun was directly above my head, and pounded its hot rays into my sweaty skull, taunting me to drop out on the spot. The final four miles on Olympic were a relentless false flat incline. Suddenly, the course took a sharp

13

left onto Flower Street, an even steeper grade, but fueled by pain and passion, I switched gears and sprinted up the hill to the finish line. My heart beat in my throat over the final 100 feet of the race, I had crushed my previous time by thirteen minutes, and again felt like I could leap across the skyscrapers towering overhead. The final six miles were torturous, and I'm glad that course is gone now. Ending a marathon uphill is simply cruel.

Later, when I was driving home on the 10 freeway, talking with my super-fast runner friend Hadara (we could talk on cell phones while driving back then), I felt serene, not exhausted. This meant L.A. would certainly not be my last marathon. I was already looking forward to training and racing for number three.

Marathon #3 – The San Francisco Marathon, 2003

Little Sister Heaven

I ran my third marathon on July 27, 2003 in San Francisco, California after receiving an invitation from my brother Peter. I had spent the last few months after the L.A. marathon in a blissful haze, wondering what to do next, so when he called, I jumped at the chance to run in San Fran alongside, or maybe in front of, my big bro. Moreover, the bonus about running a marathon in San Francisco was that I would not only be hanging out with Peter, I would also be able to visit with the original marathoner in my life, our oldest brother, Tim.

All throughout my childhood I worshipped Peter and Tim. I used my tomboy personality and athletic prowess to weasel my way into many "boys only" neighborhood kickball games, and achieved the winning kick on more than one occasion, which earned me both street cred and respect from my big bros. I revered Tim because he was the oldest, and he had assumed a father figure role once my dad moved out when I was seven. He was brilliant in school, mature beyond his years, and he laughed at all of my jokes. Tim was also the

15

first runner I looked up to. He ran cross-country and track in high school, which made him a superhero in my eyes. I remember when he would come home from a run and sit in a wicker chair in our family room, sweating into the cushion. I thought he was both badass and disgusting.

"Tim, go take a shower. You're sweating everywhere."

"Relax, Tar, I need to cool down and wait until I stop sweating before I take a shower."

It took me years to figure out that logic. But, if Tim said so, it was so.

Meanwhile, Peter was more of my playmate than an authoritative big brother. We would play football, baseball, soccer, basketball, you name it, in our back yard, front yard and side yard for hours every day for years. Our rules for basketball were that he would have to make ten baskets of two points each up to twenty points to win, and I just had to make one basket of two points to win. No joke. These were our legitimate rules. He won a lot, but I won most of the time, and we laughed every time we played.

Peter and I were both natural athletes, so it was a dream come true for us to be teammates on the cross-country team the year that was my freshman year and his senior year. He was our captain and fastest runner. I didn't really want to run, but when he asked me to join the team, I leaped out of my skin, and quickly became the "Rising Star Rookie." During our final race of the season I was running in the varsity heat, and over the last three quarters of a mile was closing in on securing a top twenty finish. That meant I would be "All League," one of the top twenty fastest runners in the five schools making up our League. It was a very cool feat for any runner, but especially for a freshman.

Over the final mile of the course, I pounded down the last hill right behind a rival runner, my entire body covered in dusty sweat as I hunted her down. Just before I turned left toward the last straightaway, I saw and heard Peter yelling and cheering for me from behind the plastic barricades, "Take her, T! Go! GO!" My heart exploded with pride and adrenaline as I surged past the runner ahead of me, pumping my arms and holding my breath as I crossed over the finish line in 20th place! I was ecstatic, but Peter lost his mind! He ran over to me and hugged me like I was a prizefighter! I felt both his love as a brother and his respect as a runner.

Unfortunately, I had a growth spurt between my freshman and sophomore year in high school which slowed my running speed way down. I grew more than three inches, going from a spritely 5'7" to a 5'10.5" behemoth. I started my sophomore season noticeably slower than I had been the year before, and it worsened as the weeks went on. Peter was away in college, but Tim had free time that summer after graduating from college and before he started his new job, so he volunteered at our week-long cross-country camp. He had already run a few marathons himself, so he was a fantastic addition to our coaching staff. I was excited going into camp, because I wanted to show off my speedy self to Tim. However, right away I discovered my newfound height was slowing me down.

I felt like such a disappointment to Tim and myself. During one of our final workouts of the week, I was farther back than ever, and burst into tears after the workout was over. Tim walked with me away from the group and let me explode. "What is wrong with me?" I said.

"It's okay, T. You're a whole lot taller this year, so it's understandable that you're a little slower."

Nope, it wasn't okay. Not to me. Running slowly in front of Tim was torture, but I was relieved to have him with me during such an ordeal. I went on to finish the season never once running in a varsity race. I promised myself that one day I would make Tim as proud of me as Peter had been that day at League Finals. My brothers' approval meant everything to me.

The night before the San Francisco Marathon, Peter's friends came over to his apartment on Haight Street to pump us up, and I was in "cool kid heaven". Peter's friends were seasoned Ironman triathletes, the ultimate level of endurance athlete in my mind, so to be in their presence was like being a ball boy swinging a bat with Babe Ruth. The Ironman is a triathlon that consists of a 2.4-mile swim, a 112-mile bike ride, and 26.2-mile run. That's right, they end their day running a marathon. I didn't say much the whole night, but even in my mute state, I felt a sense of calm because I had a bit of experience under my belt, having already finished two marathons. Still, no matter how many times you do it, 26.2 miles is a long way to go.

The car ride to the race was hysterical; Peter and I laughed the whole way there. We were both nervous, but more excited than anything. I knew a bit more than he did about what lay ahead, but I would hurt just as much. Moreover, it felt wonderful that we were in it together.

We found a great parking spot, stret
and before I knew it the gun went off, a
disappeared in the crowd. I loved the early
because we ran through the Embarcadero, the b   ..etch
of dock along the bay, then up a short, curvy hill ..ito the trees
of the Presidio. Then there was a whole lot of up, down, and
around the dizzying hills of San Francisco. I felt okay, not too
good, not too bad, until I hit the out-and-back strip of strand
around mile thirteen. Suddenly, I saw Peter again, and noticed
that he was feeling it, too when he yelled in a joking, but
strained voice, "We're running a marathon, huh?"

My spirits picked up when we ran out of Golden Gate
Park down Haight Street and were cheered on by the heavy
crowds lining both sides of the street, at least ten people deep.
Then, near the bottom of Haight Street, just before Divisidero
Street, I heard my name chanted in powerful unison: "Go
Taryn!" Peter's Ironman buddies were yelling together on the
stoop of his apartment. I felt like I was flying—I was running
downhill, had covered more than half the course, the sun was
shining, and my heroes were cheering me on. Amazing.

The next few miles of the race were awful, though: there
were no trees and barely any crowd, but there were plenty of
Reservoir Dogs-like warehouses that made me feel isolated and
annoyed. It was a classic "valley" in the many peaks and
valleys that we runners accept as part of the journey of the
marathon. One moment you are feeling invincible, even fast,
and then the next moment your stomach feels like it is being
strangled, wanting nothing more than to explode, and eject all

the sugary, goo-like chemical-energy-infused substances that it has been forced to ingest all morning. This is an excruciating reality that happens at least once or forty-five times during a race. Thankfully, a beacon of hope appeared in the form of a large crowd holding paper cups filled with the most magical of all elixirs, water. I snatched a cup in haste from a do-gooder volunteer, chugged it, then dumped the rest of the water over my head, and as if it was a baptismal miracle, I was able to run hard again.

When I came up to the mile twenty-three mark, I was sick of running, and just ready for the race to be over. I had run far enough, had drunk too much, and was ready to stop and walk for a few minutes. My stomach bulged and my feet ached from the constant pounding they took from my 150-pound frame. My head hurt, and I was hot. My desire to run quickly was losing the battle to exhaustion and hopelessness, but then I saw a hint of the Promised Land: Giants Stadium, less than a mile up ahead. I realized the finish line was close, so I picked up my pace from a pathetic jog and started to run. Thankfully, with the help of a smattering of fans along the last stretch of the course, I bolted through the final mile on my wounded legs, running as hard as I could toward the finish line.

As I entered into the final corner, I noticed a J. Crew-type guy yelling my name, and when my exhaustion cleared, tears formed because my ultimate fan was Tim! I had never seen him so excited—he was flapping his arms, and jumping up and down, acting opposite his normal calm, cool and collected self. After I crossed the finish line, he reached out and grabbed me to give me a huge hug, and kept saying that I should really be proud of myself because I had run under four hours. "Only real runners go under four hours, Taryn."

Next, I walked up farther through the finish area looking for Peter, and found him sitting on a curb, eating a banana and drinking some water.

"How did it go?" I said.

"It was rough, T."

"What was your time?'

"I think I came in around 3:40."

"Wow, that's amazing, Pete!"

"Thanks, how did you do?"

"Okay, I PR'd by fourteen minutes."

"What?"

"Yeah, I finished in 3:55."

"Tar, that's awesome, congratulations!"

"Here, let's go find Tim, I saw him at the finish line."

"Oh sweet. I didn't see him earlier."

I was in little sister heaven standing at the finish line between Peter and Tim that day because we were not just runners anymore, but marathon runners. I could tell by the tone of their voice and stance as they talked that neither one of them would ever run another marathon; it hurt them too much. Meanwhile, something very different was going on inside of me. I felt energized and alive, like my body was thanking me instead of scolding me. It felt like a rebirth, like running marathons was what I was born to do.

The following morning I went on a recovery run, and the wheels started turning in my head. I kept repeating Tim's words over and over about finishing under four hours, and what that meant for me. The logical next step was the Boston Marathon. I had never even considered it until Tim said those words, "real runner", with such pride in his voice. I started thinking about the qualifying times for Boston. I was twenty-three years old, so I would need to hit 3:40 or below in order to qualify. I thought that slicing off fifteen minutes would be a huge ask of myself, but then I remembered Peter had finished within 3:40, and that if he could do it, I could do it. It really was not that crazy of an idea; I had lopped off thirty minutes from my first marathon time two years prior, so what was another measly fifteen minutes? I decided my next goal was to qualify for the Boston marathon by the time I turned twenty-five.

Tim, Peter, Me and Mary at my high school graduation

Taryn Spates

Marathon #4 – The Dublin Marathon, 2003

Running In My Homeland

It is hard to believe now that I ran my fourth marathon in Dublin, Ireland, but I did. When I touched down back in L.A. after the San Francisco Marathon in late July, my top priority was to find a race that was on the Boston qualifying "hot list," a.k.a. flat and/or downhill courses. I wanted to allow myself some time, but I also did not have a whole lot of time on my hands since I had dropped the gauntlet to qualify by twenty-five, so when I read about the Tucson Marathon being fast, I signed up right away. Plus, it was the first weekend in December, which meant I had plenty of time to train. I was inspired and ready to get after it.

As the months ticked by, I was living the SoCal dream, living in a beach house with a wonderful roommate and working in the coolest job on the planet, but as with all my jobs in freelance production, once the project ended, so did my job security. However, since I was a hip, newly twenty-four-year-old single girl with some change in my pocket and no responsibilities but my own, I used my newfound freedom to find out if there was a marathon in Ireland anytime soon. I had been infatuated with Ireland and everything Irish ever since I realized my name was Taryn Patrick Kelly and my hair was orange. Plus, my half-birthday is St. Patrick's Day, which makes him my patron saint, and I have always been afflicted by a deep dependence on and lust for potatoes.

Much to my delight, one late afternoon in early October while trolling the marathon sites on the Internet, I found the Dublin Marathon, and it was only three weeks away! I bought a cheap ticket on the Irish airline Aer Lingus, called in some favors from friends and family for contacts I might stay with, and registered for the race, which would take place on October 27, 2003. I viewed the race as another "long run" for my ramp up to the Tucson Marathon, which was my "A" race of the year, but I could not turn down this opportunity to run a marathon in my ancestors' homeland.

On my last day of work, I drove from Playa Del Rey down to my dad's house in Palos Verdes to visit Pete and his new girlfriend, Alexa. Peter had been infatuated with Alexa for years. Over time they had developed a wonderful friendship, and I knew that she was the one for my dear, sweet, creative brother Peter. In fact, I had been visiting Peter the weekend in November in 2001 that had kicked off their friendship and eventual relationship. We had gone to Kel's Bar in the North Beach neighborhood of San Francisco, and Alexa was there with her friends. But she was outgoing, thankfully, and Peter's smile said it all. He was smitten. It would take another year and a half before they got their act together and started dating, but once they did, that was it. Naturally, she and I hit it off right away, which made me excited to spend time with them both before I took off on my great Irish running adventure! When I told them about my plan to race the Dublin Marathon, they thought it was nutty but very cool, and looked forward to hearing all the crazy stories when I got home.

The day of my departure was odd from the start. I received a message from the airline telling me that the flight was delayed, which I did not care too much about because it was a direct flight from Los Angeles to Dublin, and it was Wednesday. My race was on Monday, so all I cared about was making it there by the start. My dad dropped me off at the International terminal because he is awesome, and was proud that I was off on this crazy adventure on my own, but as an avid world business traveler, he thought it was a little weird that my flight was delayed. Once inside, I found my way to my spot in the check-in line, and stood still for many, many minutes. The line never moved. Finally there was some hustling and bustling up front and then the word got back to me: the flight was canceled, because the airline was on strike. "Excuse me?" I thought to myself. Never in my wildest dreams had I thought that the airline would strike. Who would? My inner leprechaun piped up, "Come on, my Irish brothers and sisters, you're better than this!" Pretty quickly after that announcement was made, we were told that Air France would try to accommodate us. "Vive la France!"

When I finally lurched my way up to the front of the line and listened to the heavily accented attendant describe my updated itinerary, my heartbeat quickened because they could only get me to Paris. From there, supposedly, a flight from my defunct airline would fly me to Dublin. "Um, isn't Aer Lingus on strike?" I nervously thought to myself, but I took my chances and hopped on the plane to Paris.

When we arrived at Charles De Gaulle airport, it felt cold and desolate like the French filmmaker Chris Marker's film *La Jette*, a 1962 black-and-white French film, composed of only still frames, except for one scene when a girl blinks her eyes. It is a stunning film, and that was exactly how I felt—stunned. Fortunately, my spirits picked up when I befriended a family who was also looking for the Aer Lingus counter, but when the tram dropped us off at the terminal, it was a ghost town. Panic washed over me. How was I going to get to Dublin?

I left my newfound friends, who had a plan of their own, while I headed back to the main terminal to plead with my friends at Air France. I tried to channel my pint-size high school French teacher, Mrs. Copple, when I reached the front of the line to speak with an Air France agent, but I am no polyglot. It felt like the Atlantic Ocean of misunderstanding between us. All I understood from the airline representative's sexy yet incomprehensible accent was that there was one flight I could take to Dublin, but I would have to pay for the only seat left, which was in business class. "Ha!" I almost burst out laughing, because I was unemployed with no job on the horizon. In fact, this trip had only been possible because the flight I booked was cheap. I stepped away from the counter and walked outside to the main terminal to call my dad. He listened to me, and then told me that I needed to "figure it out." That sounded a little harsh; I was his youngest child trapped in a non-English speaking country, but I heard faith in his tone, so with a renewed fire in my belly I decided to go to another Air France agent and plead my case.

I am certain that my voice wavered, but I tried to keep it together as I explained my plight, my heart in my throat, to a stunning lady dressed in an Air France uniform. She was really an angel. She listened intently to every word, and called numerous important people on her spiffy non-numbered phone, but her Herculean efforts were not looking good. Admitting defeat, I dropped my head and was turning toward the agent who had offered the business class ticket when my Air France Angel pulled my right arm back in a very Truffaut-like fashion and said that she had got me on a flight with no extra charge! I hugged her inappropriately as we both laughed out loud in victory, but there was no time to celebrate. I had to run to the gate at that instant in order to make the flight. Even though that detour to France was not planned, it was a welcome surprise to see the Eiffel Tower lit up from the airplane window as I was finally airborne and headed to Ireland.

The next few days were wonderful as I discovered Dublin by foot; I was home. I shared in some amazing family time with my sister-in-law's good friend Wendy and her family in the nearby quaint town of Greystones, just an hour or so south of Dublin. Wendy's husband Ross brought home "fish and chips" for dinner which, even as a mostly-vegetarian, I gobbled up and adored, then eagerly washed down with a pint of Guinness. The following day, I went for a quick forty-minute run before Wendy drove me back to Dublin.

Over the next two days, I was treated to a play, a trip to

Taryn Spates

Sugarloaf Mountain, and a visit to the town of Glendolough in the Irish countryside with another family friend, an Irish judge named Mary Ellen. Our timing was a little dicey on our drive back to the city, but luckily we made it back to Dublin in the nick of time for me to check in at the race Expo, because the marathon was the following morning.

I woke up excited, yet serene. I ate a Power Bar and a cup of coffee for breakfast. No one said a word to me in the large, crowded seating area of the hostel. I just ate, smiling, in a corner all by myself, nearly positive I was the lone marathon runner in the room. As I walked down the road a few blocks toward Trinity College, I high-fived myself because against hilarious odds, I had pulled it off. I was here in Ireland, walking toward another marathon starting line, about to enjoy a 26.2-mile running tour of Dublin with a few thousand of my Irish brothers and sisters.

The air was brisk, but the sun was out and smiling, which felt wonderful and inviting on my sensitive SoCal skin. I positioned myself mid-pack at the start, but I gained some ambition after a pit stop, and darted and jumped around runners, adjusted my pace, and settled into a comfortable groove. After about seven miles, I realized I was running faster than normal. It felt good so I didn't change a thing for as many miles as I could hang on. When I cruised through mile ten, I met my hero, and future self. Her name was Greta; she was cruising at near eight minute mile pace, was sixty years old, and this was her 35th marathon! I was so inspired; I gasped, "I want to be you when I grow up!" She smiled at me, but I probably startled her with my *big* American enthusiasm.

Oh well, I thought, she made my day!

Gratefully, I found another gear, switched up my pace again and zoomed past many pale-legged runners farther up the pack even though I was pushing myself beyond my limits. My eyelids started to twitch from the combination of sweat, water and happy tears. As the miles ticked by, the crowd got louder and louder, but I was creeping toward my red line: I was under my personal record pace, so I had to keep pushing.

The last few miles were a blur. The last half-mile the course narrowed as the crowds crept too close for comfort, but I didn't care. If I took someone out, so be it, I was not slowing down. As I saw the finish line approaching, I glanced once, twice, and may be once more at the clock to realize I had done it. I had run four minutes faster than I had in San Francisco, finishing in 3:51!! I leaped across the finish line like a lass out of *River Dance*, and screamed with glee, smiling from ear to ear. This did not qualify me for Boston, but I knew I could reach it in Tucson. I was getting closer and faster to reaching 3:40.

After the race, I showered and quickly set off on my last walkabout around the city, and enjoyed my well-deserved post-race Guinness at a bar called *Temple Bar*, in the super-hip section of Dublin called Temple Bar. Later, Mary Ellen picked me up and took me to dinner and to see a movie called *Intermission*, which was really fun, and exactly what I needed to cap off my day and my whole Irish experience. Only days before, I had felt alone when I set foot in the country, but between meeting Wendy, Mary Ellen, Greta and every kind smile I encountered on the streets, I felt part of it all. Ireland

Taryn Spates

felt like home.

Marathon #5 – The Tucson Marathon, 2003

Never Wear Red Shorts In The Desert

The events that followed after I returned from Ireland were life-altering, and not in a wonderful way. Upon my arrival back home, I regaled my roommate, Molly, with my adventures, and shared my hilarious travel woes with my family, but there was a lurking of uncertainty underneath. I was still unemployed, and my "A" race, the Tucson Marathon, was rapidly approaching.

On the night of November 3, I was chatting with Molly and her visiting uncle when my former boss and current neighbor, Shannon, came raging up our staircase and knocked on our door, yelling, "Fire! Fire!" It was surreal. We didn't panic, but the next two minutes felt like two hours, as if time had ground to a halt and we were moving in slow motion. Shannon grabbed my computer and launched us out of our front door. From the safety of the street, I saw flames licking the unit above ours, our landlord's unit, where the fire had started. The firefighters swooped in with lightning-fast heroics, but the unit was gone. Our unit was spared any fire damage, but it was waterlogged and uninhabitable. We ended up staying at my parents' house that night and a couple nights thereafter, much to my dad's chagrin. The invitation was not indefinite; Molly and I needed to figure out what to do next. My gut was telling me to find a place of my own.

Over the next few weeks, my stress levels were at Mach Twelve! Miraculously, I lined up a short-term dream job as an assistant at a production company on The Lot in West Hollywood. The gig did not last long, but during the few weeks I was there I fell in love with the glorious people and neighborhoods of West Hollywood, so at the first opportunity, I snatched up a studio apartment one block south of the Sunset Strip. I was set to move in on New Year's Eve.

Meanwhile, I had the most important race of my life to train for. The Tucson course is ranked as the one of the top Boston qualifier courses because it is virtually downhill, which all but guarantees a fast time. On Saturday December 6, I boarded a Southwest airlines flight out of Burbank to Tucson. The cab ride from the airport was expensive, much more than I planned for, but the hotel was all I dreamed it would be. The expo event before the race was unique because, for the first time, I walked around the hotel ballroom with a Cheshire Cat grin, like I had the winning hand of poker in my grip. I felt primed for the race, calm even, and ready to blow the doors off of the desert come dawn the next morning.

However, cockiness overwhelmed common sense when I decided to eat pasta at the athlete welcome dinner, an amateur move with disastrous consequences. The meal was tasty, sure, but it had no business being in my belly the night before the most important marathon of my life. Next came a sleepless night, merely annoying on any other night, but detrimental this time because I needed to be up and out of my room by 4:00 a.m. to make the bus that drove us 26.2 miles into the dark desert sky to the starting line.

The desert morning was cold, so the race organizers let us sit on the bus long after we arrived at the start in order to keep us warm. But they kept us on the buses for too long. I was bouncing off the walls, trying to get my fellow runners pumped up, which felt fun to me, but it might have been obnoxious to everyone else. Oh well, I was ready to run. Once off the bus, I hit up the port-o-let as usual, but my stomach was still restless. It was cold, but majestic, because we were literally in the middle of the desert; there were no spectators, just us marathoners pointed in one direction, downhill, to the finish line.

When the gun went off, I shot out like a cannonball. The miles ticked by quickly, but something was wrong. My stomach was seizing up. The pain pierced my abdomen, but regardless of my torture, I had to push; I wanted so badly to make my splits for my 3:40 qualifying time, which meant no time for pit stops. I had to keep running.

Once I passed the mile nine marker, I knew my dream of a sub 3:40 finish was over. My quads were bursting from the constant pounding of the tantalizing downhill course and my stomach was screaming at me to stop. Suddenly, my day switched from personal record pursuit to survival. I was doubled over in pain and could not spot another port-o-let up ahead, so I made a gruesome choice for my own salvation. I will spare you the details, but I will say that I had to pull over on the side of the non-shaded, wide-open highway to ease my pain, and that I regretted wearing red shorts.

Nevertheless, I kept running, with stops at every port-o-let stop on the course, but I finished the race. I had no support team with me that day, which was a blessing, because I would have failed them all. I was embarrassed and angry at the finish line, even though I had accomplished another huge feat of finishing a marathon in the respectable time of 4:15. Considering my bodily breakdown, that was commendable, but it was far from what I set out to do. I felt like my day, and my dream to qualify for Boston was ruined.

I held onto my "not-so-cheery" attitude through my hurried clean-up routine in my fancy hotel room, then caught another expensive cab ride back to the airport. I called Peter to fill him in on my devastating day. He was great as always, but it still felt like a nightmare I wished I could wake up from.

A few hours later, while sitting alone waiting for my plane to board, I met a fellow marathoner and confided in him the details of my race. I expected him to lament in my misery, but instead he threw out the best line ever. "Oh, you had G.I problems. That happens." That was what I needed to hear. Shit happens.

I knew I had a storm of turmoil awaiting me at home, but I had faith that I would figure it out. It was only December of 2003, I still had nine months before my deadline of qualifying for Boston. I had time, and now I had real experience to build on. I had learned important lessons in Tucson: 1. No pasta dinners, 2. No "downhill" courses. 3. No quitting.

Marathon #6 – The Palos Verdes Marathon, 2004

Meeting the One

Right out of the gate, the year 2004 brought some *big* changes in my life. I finally had some great production gigs again; in fact I was awarded my first ever full-time job as a Production Coordinator at a visual effects facility called Digital Dimension. This may not seem like a huge accomplishment to the average worker-bee, but for someone who had only worked freelance her entire adult life, a staff position was a bank-account-building dream come true.

Furthermore, during my first hour on the job, my life took a gigantic left turn. While walking out of the kitchen toward my new office, I noticed a guy walking down the hallway wearing orange cargo pants, a black beanie, and Camper dress shoes, flanked by two guys on either side of him who were hanging on his every word. I quickly learned from my boss that the snazzily dressed fellow was named Marion Spates.

Marion was a 3D artist and production manager, and since I was the production coordinator in charge of moving the projects along, we worked together closely every day.

After a couple of months, I noticed Marion frequently visiting my office, on both official and unofficial business. During our many chats, I learned he was from Texas, that his nickname until he was about twenty-one was Butch, and that he was divorced and had a five-year-old daughter named Hannah. He gushed about Hannah constantly. He was everyone's favorite at work because he was funny, gregarious and kind. Soon I was racing to work early so we could talk by ourselves in the kitchen before our co-workers arrived. Mind you, Marion was not my type at all. He had earrings, tattoos and a ridiculous haircut. He was ten years older than me, divorced, and a father, (gulp!), but his kindness trumped all of that. I knew Marion would change my life forever.

Throughout all of my heart-fluttering fun at work, I was training for my sixth marathon, a hometown jaunt in Palos Verdes. I was not taking this race seriously as a Boston qualifier because the course was incredibly hilly, a total time crusher, but I thought it would serve as a nice long run to get me out of my Tucson funk. The Palos Verdes Marathon is a very small race in terms of participants, but it literally goes by my parents' front yard, which was not by chance on my part. I wanted a built-in support team for this race. My bruised ego needed it, and Dad and Sally did not disappoint.

I did not break any land speed records with that race. It was by far the toughest course I ever conquered, which was satisfying enough, because I finished feeling better than expected. I was ready to shake off Tucson for good, and find a new marathon that would serve as another shot at qualifying for Boston.

Marathon #7 – The Sacramento Cow Town Marathon, 2004

Finally, Boston

Marion and I started dating officially on September 19, 2004, just two days after my twenty-fifth birthday, and two weeks before marathon number seven, the Cow Town Marathon in Sacramento, California. We had been friends for months so he was well aware that I was a runner and that I was fanatical about qualifying for Boston. He even knew what time I needed to finish in order to do it; in fact, he left me a message at 10:40 a.m. on Sunday October 3, the day of the marathon, saying, "Hi, it is 10:40, so hopefully you have finished by now, and if you did, you qualified for Boston!" I was already smitten at that point, but that message was like Cupid's arrow straight through my slow-beating heart.

I had flown up to Sacramento the day before the race; it is a quick flight from L.A., and far easier on the legs than the five-hour drive in the car. I rented a gigantic Lincoln or something—picture your grandparents' last fly ride—and that is what I was rolling around our state's capital in. My hotel was nothing special, barely a hotel at all actually, but it would do for the purpose of this trip. The race expo was simple and efficient, which I appreciated. The last thing I needed was another energy gel.

My pre-race nutrition was still in its beta phase, so I slurped a huge vitamin-infused smoothie and forearm-sized brownie for lunch, then treated myself to a box of Junior Mints later that night while I watched the movie *Ladder 49*, starring John Travolta and Joaquin Phoenix. Next, I took my luxurious vehicle on a tour of the course. Before I went to bed, I knocked back some trail mix and Gatorade, which was not the perfect pre-race meal, but it hit the spot. I slept soundly, which was a blessing considering my rabid nerves and that the hotel was right next to a busy highway, but come dawn I bounced out of bed primed and ready to run.

The starting line was at a park in the middle of a suburban neighborhood, and the crowd was on the small side, which I loved. I nodded and smiled while milling around before the gun went off, knowing today would be more than just a race that awarded my seventh finishing T-shirt. It felt special.

I started off as planned, running at a faster pace than I needed in order to meet my qualifying time. That was perfect because it meant I was banking time for when I really needed it later in the race. The course weaved through neighborhoods lined with bulging, leaf-heavy trees, which meant lots of shade underneath nature's umbrella, a runner's dream conditions. The only not-so-scenic section was the stretch between miles twelve and fourteen on the frontage road to the freeway, but I did not think much of the ugliness because I was way ahead of my qualifying pace at the halfway mark. I was ecstatic, but I tried to keep my emotions in check and execute each mile to perfection.

My energy started to wane a bit around mile seventeen, the norm for me, but just before I let my head droop too low, I glimpsed out of the corner of my eye a gorgeous couple galloping across the park yelling their beautiful faces off: "Go Taryn!!!" I cheered back with a smile because these gorgeous fanatics were my friends Sarah and Mike! They had come to the race to surprise me because Sarah knew how important qualifying for Boston was to me. She had been there cheering me on for my first marathon in San Diego, and knew that I was betting the house on this race for it to finally happen.

Sarah is an amazing human being; she was the first friend I made my freshman year in college, and is a pediatric nurse today. I am very thankful to have her in my life. I will never forget meeting her. It was only two days after I moved in to my freshman dorm in Libby Hall at the University of Colorado at Boulder, my parents were already on their long drive home and my roommate had yet to arrive because I had to come early for Orientation. I was talking with Peter on the phone with my door closed, feeling freaked out, and he said, "Open your door." I was so nervous, but I opened my door and let college in. About thirty minutes after I opened my door, I saw this thin, short-haired gorgeous girl swoosh past my door in a nervous hurry. I leaped off my bed and yelled out of the door, "Hi!" She lived two doors down but stopped cold in her tracks to say "Hi" back, and we have been friends ever since.

Sarah had clutch timing finding me at mile seventeen because I needed some pep in my step at that moment of the race, and she and Mike gave me the jolt I needed to keep pushing my pace. I was so close to both finishing the race and qualifying for Boston. She told me that my younger sister Sarah, along with Tim and his family were waiting for me at the finish line.

The final mile of the course looped around the park toward the finish so I could see it about half a mile before I made the last turn. I heard the announcer reading off times, I looked at my watch. It read 3:35. I had done it! I would finish under 3:40! My official time was 3:37. At last, I had punched my ticket for Boston! Tim was the first person to come up and tell me that I qualified, which made it extra special.

Above all, I was impressed with my execution. I had done what I needed to do, even after three attempts at qualifying for Boston after my San Francisco "qualify by twenty-five" goal. I had done it, and would be running the Boston marathon in six months. I could not wait to call Marion and ask if he wanted to come with me to Boston…and everywhere else for the rest of my life.

We all ate a delicious Mexican meal in downtown Sacramento after I cleaned up and checked out of the hotel. Then I said my goodbyes to my amazing cheering squad and ordered myself a Guinness at a local bar while killing time before my flight. Since Dublin, I had figured this would be my new marathon finishing tradition. I sat quietly drinking my precious Irish brew and gave myself an internal high-five, satisfied that I had conquered my goal, and giddy that my next Guinness would be in Boston.

Taryn Spates

Marathon #8 – The Boston Marathon, 2005

Be Careful What You Wish For

The six months in between the Sacramento Cow Town Marathon, my Boston Marathon qualifier, and *The* Boston Marathon were split between spending time with Marion and working. I did maintain my marathon fitness, but my "Boston Marathon Qualifying" fitness disappeared somewhere around Thanksgiving. Moreover, I came down with a chest-scorching case of pneumonia just before Christmas that was both painful and humbling. I could not run at all for about ten days because my lungs were filled with liquid sickness that felt like piercing daggers every time I tried to do more than walk. Somewhere around mid-January I started healing up and getting my act together, but when marathon weekend rolled around, I was not in the prime shape I wanted to be.

After years of pursuing my goal, the third weekend in April finally arrived. Marion and I were ready to board the plane to Boston. As I was sitting in front of our gate, I saw many passengers wearing BAA jackets (The Boston Athletic Association is the governing body that organizes the marathon). I smiled because soon I would be able to wear one, too. I felt calm and content sitting among my people. I had worked as hard or harder as they had in order to catch this flight, but speed didn't matter. We were all Boston qualifiers, and that was enough.

I had decided a month earlier, in the in depths of the planning process, to rent a minivan because we thought we would need it to drive my friends around who were flying in from Colorado. I spent so much time and effort prepping for this race and I did not want to miss a beat. I had a solid crew lined up: my dad, Sally, Peter, Alexa, and my girls from Boulder— Chanda, Annie, and Hillary. Peter and Alexa shared a room with us, which brought about some serious bonding (and slight discomfort), but for the most part it was fun. Dad and Sally were in the same hotel as us, the Hyatt Regency in Cambridge, but my girls were staying at a swanky spot smack dab in the middle of the city. In any other circumstance, I would have been right there with them, bar-hopping and laughing together all over the city. But a) I was with my future husband, and, b) I was in town to run the most prestigious marathon in the world, so I needed to keep my mind and body clean, clear and focused.

We ended up only using the minivan a handful of times; I took Marion with me to drive the course on the Saturday before the race, which in our "soccer mom" rental was decadent and very comfortable. We drove the course in reverse starting from the finish line in Boston and driving west 26.2 miles to the starting line in Hopkinton. The course was gorgeous but a tad startling for Marion.

46

"Are you really going to run this far?"

"Yep."

It is true that 26.2 miles in a straight line seems pretty far, but that distance always feels longer sitting in a car than running on two feet. Plus, I would be jacked up on adrenaline come race day, and sharing the road with thousands of fellow runners and rabid fans, making the miles disappear quicker than they do from behind a windshield. I was happy that he was able to experience the course with me, and would therefore have a deeper understanding of where I was throughout the day. Also, I think he fell in love with my badassery a bit more during that drive; his bewildered gaze was a dead giveaway of his newfound respect for my running prowess. I was nervous, but excited. The race was finally here and I was actually in Boston driving the course. It felt surreal, but it was real. The next time I would see these trees, leaves, and land would be as I ran along them on my own two feet.

The morning of Monday April 18 started early, but really didn't need to. The gun went off at 12 noon, but I needed to be downtown to catch my bus by 7 a.m. The streets were lined with yellow school buses as far as my eyes could see. We runners were loading up and heading one way toward Hopkinton. I sat next to a woman in her mid-forties who was a bubbly ball of energy because her daughter would be watching her run a marathon for the first time. I thought in that instant that I would love to run this race with Hannah one day, maybe when she was twenty-five? I would be forty-four, so totally do-able. Ah, a "someday-in-the-future" stepmom can dream.

I waved goodbye to my maternal seat buddy once I walked off the bus and turned toward the port-o-let line, my top priority of the day. All of us were ambling around the athletic fields at Hopkinton High School, waiting nervously for the minutes to pass before we were allowed to line up at the starting line. I found my happy place, sitting and stretching inside a big tent where I met a few excited folks, all of us psyching each other up for the life-altering afternoon ahead.

Finally, just before 12, we lined up in our corrals, which were sorted by qualifying time. It was me and a bunch of other sub 3:40 runners, but these girls looked far too serious for my liking. I wanted to yell, "Ladies, we're here! The hard part is over—let's just go out and enjoy the day!" Luckily, I resisted my jovial urge and simply shouldered up alongside them in silence. I felt out of place. I was out of shape, embarrassed by my solid light pink outfit, and generally disappointed in myself. However, my "pity party" balloons popped with the crack of the gun. We were off. Ready or not, it was time to run!

The first few miles were fast -- too fast for my comfort level -- but a whole lot of fun! It felt like an all-out sprint on the way to the swing set after lunch in elementary school, and the cheers and density of the crowds were insane! There were people at least ten feet deep on both sides of the street for miles. It felt like a parade; the people of Boston lived up to the hype.

I reined in my pace around mile five or so as I started running up and down hills that looked easy from afar but stung a bit once up close and personal. I was enjoying myself,

48

but something was off. I was happy to be finally running this race, reaching my goal of qualifying and racing by twenty-five, but I kept thinking about how Marion was faring alone with my parents, Peter and Alexa. We had been together for a while by now, but he had never spent this much time, or any time alone, with my family, thus spurring my nervous stomach around mile twelve. Just as my head started to hang low and my legs began to drag, I felt a thunderous, steady stream of screaming from a half-mile up ahead. It was the unison siren calls from the all-female students of Wellesley College. The college is located between miles twelve and thirteen on the course, the perfect spot to pick up the spirits of those of us not having the best race of our lives, because their cheers transformed us into champions. I drank in their energy, gave a couple high-fives, and started to *really* run again.

The next few miles were interspersed with pockets of quickness, surrounded by unrelenting slow motion. My self-esteem hit an all-time low when I heard a runner in front of me talking on her cell phone and reporting that the first female had already finished the race. Meanwhile, I was only halfway through. Next, I took a sharp left turn on the course and felt the warmth of mid-afternoon sunshine; it was a little after 2 p.m. at this point, and it felt weird to be running so late in the day, but I took a deep breath, gathered the whispers of my integrity and pushed on.

Soon enough I found myself at mile seventeen, the base of Heartbreak Hill. I had been told that Heartbreak Hill was a steep hill, but no one mentioned how long it was, and honestly, I never researched it. I have my ignorance to blame, but the "Hill" goes on for four miles! No joke: it starts at mile seventeen, leads up a twisty road and finally crests at mile twenty-one right in front of Boston College. To be honest, I am being a tad overdramatic here. Heartbreak Hill is actually the last and steepest of the Newton hills, which are about four solid rollers, but nothing earth-shattering. I was simply unprepared. I was annoyed with the never-ending climb, but thrilled beyond belief when I heard, then saw Marion, Dad, Sally, Peter and Alexa cheering for me at the top. I was relieved that Marion was still alive. In fact, they looked like they were genuinely enjoying each other's company. It was a marathon miracle.

Unfortunately, at my current pace, I had a good forty-five minutes left of running before I would cross the finish line. I ran as hard as I could, smiling at the crowd with every ounce of excitement and passion I had left, and continued on until I rounded the left corner onto Boylston Street and charged into the finish chute. I finished with a time of 4:11 hours, thirty-four minutes slower than my qualifying time in Sacramento. *Ugh.*

I strained my exhausted eyeballs looking for my family while I waited for what felt like an eternity in the "Family Meeting" area to be reunited with my motley crew. But they were stuck in the train from their last spectating spot on Heartbreak Hill, missing my finish completely. I later found out that my friends had slept in too late, and didn't risk missing their flight to cheer for me on the course. *Classic.*

As I waited for my family, my disappointment started to fade away because even though the race itself was abysmal, I had accomplished my goal of running the Boston Marathon by the age twenty-five, a victory indeed. Also, I remembered that the hard part was getting to the race. Running it was the cherry on top.

Taryn Spates

Marathon #9 – The Santa Clarita Marathon, 2005

Backyard Racing

I have a special place in my heart for the Santa Clarita Marathon. For starters, it is close to my house, and anything that is geographically desirable in L.A. — meaning less than a thirty-minute drive — is worth its weight in gold. Most of my marathons require months of planning, hotels, flights, car rentals, food choices, etc., but Santa Clarita is essentially in my backyard, which gives it a gold star in my book. I ran the race on November 6, 2005, a little over six months after Boston. I signed up because of its location, and I figured enough time had passed since my heart-wrenching race in Beantown and I would have enough time to regain my pre-pneumonia fitness.

Unfortunately, I was still not ready to climb out of my "Why am I such a #$*&&% runner?" state of mind. I trained enough to run it, but once again I was not in proper marathon shape on the starting line. On the life front, Marion and I were engaged, living together, and in the early stages of planning our wedding. It was an exciting time, kind of, but more nauseating and stressful than I ever thought it would be.

Nevertheless, training for the marathon was my escape and lifeline, but for the first time it also felt more like a distraction.

I showed up on race day nervous for the approaching pain I would feel all day. My ego promised me this was not my first marathon, but my heart and body felt like I was back as a beginner. The race was not large, but reasonable enough to feel competitive and proud to be a part of it. The gun went off just after the sun peeked over the starting line, then we turned west up a hill and into the darkness of early morning shade cascading across Valencia Avenue. I ran with short breath because I was already winded; I wasn't tired but insecure about my disjointed pace that kept knocking the wind out of me. Once we crested the hill just after the mile 1 marker, I exhaled, opened up my stride, and enjoyed the long downhill right turn where I stopped thinking about my pace and just let my body move.

The next ten miles of the course covered various warehouse-laden streets and repeating tract-home neighborhoods that taunted my motivation. I wished I could have taken the right turn at the sign, "Half Marathoners This Way". Alas, I ran past that sign toward another 13.1 fun-filled miles of gorgeous urban sprawl.

The course traveled along a bike path for most of the back half of the marathon up and down a few hills, but nothing close to the climb just after the start. My legs were daydreaming of the days long ago when I made them a priority and worked them into the shape they deserved. Instead, I was taking advantage of them and forcing them to carry me 26.2 miles in a selfish attempt to change my mood. I cursed my lack of discipline to train properly for this marathon, but I was in it, and had to get through it.

Soon after I ran past the fifteen-mile marker I started to pick up my pace then heard a booming, "Go Taryn!" yelled out from a zooming car. It was Marion. He and Hannah had rallied out of bed early to cheer me on. A surge of pride flooded my veins and I smiled wide, knowing my team had arrived.

The sun was high and hot by 9:45 a.m. when I was running across the bubbling asphalt out-and-back section between miles nineteen and twenty-three. I tried to keep my focus on my pace and the path ahead, but I couldn't help drifting over and noticing the despair and exhaustion dripping across the other runners going past me in the opposite direction. I longed to be the ones already on their way home, and felt pity for those I saw behind me; it was a clinic on self-composure.

The final two miles were grotesque. I wanted it to be over; my heart was simply someplace else. Then I made the last left turn toward the finish chute and was flanked by roaring crowds cheering on both sides of the street. I was in tears from all of the love, but I was spent. I crossed the line overwhelmed with disappointment and wished I could take it all back and run it again. The medal slung around my neck felt heavy. I wanted to give it back. Instead, I just walked toward my "soon to be family" and let them be proud of me.

I resolved to myself while stuffing my face with pizza, cookies and ice cream at my post-marathon celebratory lunch that I needed a break from marathons. I was too distracted to enjoy them, and couldn't give them my full heart and attention. I wanted to fall in love with marathons all over again, and in order to do that, I had to let them go.

Marathon #10 – The Long Beach Marathon, 2006

Rough Road To The Alter

The start of 2006 exploded with promise and excitement. I was engaged, my career was thriving, but by the Ides of March, my world had crumbled around me and settled into dust at my feet. I quit my job in solidarity because of an injustice our bosses had flung at Marion. He left too, of course. We both felt that leaving Digital Dimension was a blessing in disguise because we went on to work on projects that were better suited for us. The downside was that we stopped working together, something many couples might be grateful for but I had cherished those times together. I missed working alongside him every day. Luckily, we were starting to get the ball rolling with our wedding plans, which was a needful distraction, but I craved something more.

I decided one night in June that I wanted to put another marathon on my calendar, both to keep me focused, and as motivation to whip myself into stellar wedding shape. I chose the Long Beach Marathon in early October because it was local, only taking an easy morning drive and no hotel reservations. It would be about three weeks before my wedding, which ensured that I would be "beach ready" for our honeymoon in Jamaica. I knew it would be a large race, with more than 10,000 runners for sure, but I was not concerned. This should be a fun day at the races, no pressure.

I left our apartment in North Hollywood early on race morning so I would be able to comfortably move through my pre-race routine without much distress. I know I walked around the crowds and was excited, but not much else really pops out about this race—probably because I was consumed with my wedding and everything negative that went along with it. I finished the race in 4:11, an even slower time than Santa Clarita nearly a year before. But it still felt good to run long and share the agony and ecstasy with thousands of like-minded strangers. I knew I had a lot of work to do in order to mold myself into the runner I had once been, but I wasn't upset about it. I had more present concerns to be upset about.

I would never wish on my worst enemy the kind of agony I endured during the build-up to my wedding. Marion is a wonderful person and had been from the moment I met him, but he might as well have been wearing a big scarlet letter "D" on his chest for "Divorced" as far as my family was concerned. They were only focused on the facts: he been married before, had a daughter, and was ten years older than me. I knew months before we started dating that my family would blow a gasket once they found out he was the one I wanted, but I could never have prepared myself for the hardened disapproval they had for him. The fact was that I loved Marion, and in my gut I knew my family would realize what a great match he was for me some day. So I said a prayer, gritted my teeth and moved forward with our wedding.

Fortunately, our wedding went off without a hitch. It was slightly unconventional, but perfect for us. We went skydiving and rode our motorcycles around our favorite motocross track in front of our guests, then changed into our proper wedding attire in the back of the tent company's trailer, and exchanged vows just after sunset. We danced the night away with our family and friends as they toasted to our happiness and future together. And let me tell you, that future has been pretty wonderful so far.

Marathon #11 – The Catalina Marathon, 2007

Happy Trails!

The year 2007 started with a bang because I was newly married and had finally found my dream job. The company was filled wall to wall with brilliant artists and producers who genuinely cared about their work and each other; it was a fantastic place to go to work. Then in early February, I acquiesced to Marion's pleas and agreed to start looking for a house. Naturally, in true Marion-and-Taryn fashion, we found our "perfect" house the first day we started looking. It was right in our price point, sat on a pleasant corner lot, and felt like home the moment we walked through the door. The seller asked for a sixty-day escrow, which we had no issue with because we honestly didn't know any better, and just said "yes." It turned out the extra time worked heavily in our favor. Luckily, we were able to secure financing on our own, but the process took its toll and I needed a distraction. Therefore, I signed up for my first trail marathon.

There is a small, majestic island about twenty six miles off of the California coast called Catalina. I grew up seeing it every day from my backyard, but I never thought I would run around it one day. I did, and that day was March 17, 2007. The alarm went off at 3 a.m. on race morning. Yes, you read that right, 3 a.m.! The reason for the early start was that I had to drive about an hour south to Marina Del Rey in order to catch a ferry to the start of the race at Twin Harbors on Catalina. The boat was full of nervous, sleepy runners but I did not talk to anyone. Instead, I was lulled to sleep by the rushing ocean all around us.

Soon after landing on shore, I stood in the pre-dawn darkness with the rest of the runners waiting to be ushered over a wide field to our makeshift starting line. I saw many stereotypical, grizzly runners on every side of me: older bandana-wearing men and a few women passionately embracing cotton and high-fiving each other like eight year olds. I felt like a true rookie; it was amazing. When I looked up, all I saw were hills in front of me, and a lone buffalo off to the edge of the field enjoying his breakfast and view of the many two-legged strangers in his backyard. Meanwhile, I was just happy to be there, smiling from ear to ear because I knew this was going to be a true running experience that would to shred me to the bone.

When the gun went off, runners starting cheering and yelling before starting our first of many climbs up many, many hills throughout the race. I had no delusions of starting off speedy. I was a novice with this trail business, so I wanted to be smart and just tuck into a good rhythm with the many seasoned crazies around me. We were all moving in a single-file line for the most part, up and over various trails and rocks, respecting the careful footing needed to stay upright and move along safely. I looked at my watch around mile four, and quickly decided not to do that again. I was moving at a painfully slow pace, but someone had told me for trail races to add an hour to my usual finish time, so considering that concession, I guess I was on pace. Nevertheless, I kept my head up the rest of the day.

The course was breathtaking. I had always viewed Catalina as this far-off Neverland across the ocean, and suddenly here I was running all over and around it like I was within my own sweat-infused fairytale — it was surreal. Nevertheless, the hills were relentless, so I followed my cohorts and walked up most of them, a sin in marathons, but in this case it seemed like part of the unspoken code so I went along with it.

There were a few blessed moments between miles fifteen and seventeen where we dropped down into a valley and ran along a dusty path that bordered an expansive ranch. It felt vacant, but I think the animals could have just been shy from all of us nutty runners ruining their peaceful Saturday morning. In any case, I felt their invisible energy push me along, and for the first time all day I was actually running.

The course started in Two Harbors and wound its way through to the other side of the island to Avalon, the hip hub of activity in Catalina. It felt like we were truly running into civilization because after miles and miles of pure nature, we ran up a long winding fire road, crested the top, then dipped over the other side into the bustle of Avalon. Thrilled at the sight before me, I screamed down the last hill at a scorching pace. Suddenly, a seasoned trail runner came up behind me and cheered at my performance. Obviously, he was aware of my naiveté but he was kind with his support before he blew by me down the final turn into the finish chute along Main Street.

My finish time was right on the money for the trail course prediction: 4:52. Not bad, but still a longer-than-usual day of running for me. My body had never worked that hard just to survive a course. I was very proud of my efforts, and left Catalina that afternoon with a renewed faith in what I was capable of.

Marathon #12 – Ironman Louisville, 2008

Why I Became An Ironman

I first became enamored with Ironman triathlons in the early nineties while sitting in front of our family television, mouth agape, staring at the tenacity and grit of Mark Allen running along the bubbling asphalt in Kona Hawaii at the World Championships. The race felt like a dream and unattainable to mere mortals like me, but after I ran Boston, I sank my teeth into the flesh of a new goal: becoming an Ironman.

I am sure it is not too far out to assume that it had a whole lot to do with my brother Peter. In the summer of 2003, Peter and a few of his friends decided to sign up and race Ironman Lake Placid on July 25, 2004. It is necessary to sign up for these races a year in advance because they sell out quickly, and it takes a whole year to train for them. (*I cannot stress that enough. If any of you are planning on racing an Ironman anytime in your life, you need to give your body no less than one year to prepare for such a tremendous effort.*) Peter and his cronies were all studs in their late twenties or early thirties, trying to find the time to train for an Ironman while maintaining somewhat of their "normal" lifestyle. It was a struggle and Peter felt it, but he made it through, and arrived in Lake Placid prepared to race.

My sister Mary and I decided to cheer him on along with both sets of our parents. But we were rollin' on a tight budget and missing more than one day of work was not an option, so we flew out on the red-eye on Friday night, then drove five hours through Manhattan and much of New York until we arrived at our upstate destination of mesmerizing Lake Placid.

We stayed at a huge house that Peter's friends were staying at too, and to say there was tension in the air is a colossal understatement. Mary and I bunked together in the basement, and woke up at the ridiculously early hour of 5 a.m. Mind you, this was Eastern Time and we were still on Pacific Time, which meant it was 2 a.m. for us; and we had been traveling the entire day before, so we were a little out of sorts. I think it was the first time in all the years I had known my lovely sister that she did not apply gallons of makeup on her face before beginning her day. There was simply no time for that. I am sure I was exhausted, but I did not think about my fatigue at all because I was in awe of these five or six guys and girls who were about to shatter their existence all day, swimming, biking and running. It was like standing above the dugout before game seven of the World Series and hoping one of the players would see my waves and cheers of good luck before they ran to their positions and prepared to make history. I was so happy I had made the trip.

It took tremendous reserve not to give Peter a big hug and tell him how proud I was of him for putting in the hard work to even show up to race. Instead, I gave him space. I had faith that he knew I respected what he was doing, because I secretly wished I was doing it too.

Alexa had made these hysterical matching T-shirts for all of us to wear during the race, which had Peter's bib number on the front and his nickname for each of us on the back. Mine read, "Go Hone!" because Peter had called both Mary and me "Hone Wrink" when we were growing up. I don't know where he came up with that phrase, but it stuck. In fact, he still calls me Hone Wrink to this day. The shirts were both clever and helpful because they were bright orange, so it would be easy for Peter to spot us in the crowd. When everyone was fueled up and ready to go, we followed the athletes down from the house to the shore of Mirror Lake, where there were over 2,000 athletes lined up in wetsuits and nervous expressions. It would be a tough, long, hard day for every one of them.

The start of the race was a spectacle. The serene lake erupted in whitecaps as the athletes thrashed their arms in order to move ahead in the crowd and find a good position near the front. My breathing stopped for a short eternity: I had never been so envious, and frightened, in my life. The athletes had to swim two laps around the lake to complete the 2.4 miles, and in just over an hour Peter ran out of the water and passed us on his way to the transition area. He was the first of his friends out of the water with a very impressive time that I know was super-swimmer Alexa's doing—that girl can swim, and I know she helped Peter a lot with his swim training. We quickly scrambled over to the Bike Out section of the transition area so we could see him pedal off into oblivion, otherwise known as 112 miles of upstate New York's wooded wonderland.

We all decided to get some breakfast after the swim, because he would be on the bike for more than five hours, giving us some time to kill. Over breakfast, Alexa passed out cards that Peter had written to each of us, a genuine "thank you" befitting his character. I was blown away by his card. Obviously, I still have it; it means as much to me today as it did back then. This is an excerpt of what he wrote:

What up T! I'll bet you're watching this whole spectacle wishing that you could be wearing a # on your way to the finish line. Am I right? We both seem to share the same pleasure of pushing ourselves for these long endurance races. And I think you understand the reason why I'm out here better than anyone. Which makes it that much more special for me that you're here.

He was right; I did get it, and I knew that I would be there some day. But it was his day that day, and I just wanted to cheer loud and proud for my big bro!

Peter started the run looking strong, which is an awesome feat, because the Lake Placid bike course is one of the most difficult on the Ironman circuit. But Peter is a runner above anything else, so I knew he would crush the marathon. We found a great spectating spot on top of a hill that the runners passed through four times, so we saw a lot of everybody, which was fantastic and helped the time fly by.

As a bonus, Mary and I were having the time of our lives together. She is probably my favorite person to spend an uninterrupted seventy-two hours with (a statement my mother probably strained her eyes to confirm she read correctly, but it's true). Our Ironman adventure reminded me of the only time growing up when we were not at each other's throats—playing in the ocean. It could have been because we instinctively knew we had to protect each other from the lurking danger behind every crashing wave, or that we just let ourselves go and let the power of the ocean overwhelm us and enjoy the moment. Our routine of bickering at each other would pick right up again on cue once we were back home fighting for shower position, but while in the ocean, we were in perfect sync. Mary and I are very different, yes, but she is my sister, confidante, and possibly the only person on the planet who knows every inch of me inside and out. That said, she did make me drive the whole trip—all ten hours of our commute from JFK to Lake Placid and back—but it was worth it. No one makes me feel as genuinely myself as Mary; she brings out the best in me.

Peter's last couple of miles of the marathon were a teary mess for all of us. We were all so proud of him. We knew he would do it, but witnessing someone you love finish an Ironman is truly an amazing experience, and he did it in spectacular fashion, finishing in 11:29.

Peter never raced another Ironman after Lake Placid. He asked Alexa to marry him a couple months after the race, and has been in the driver's seat of his life ever since. I was inspired by Mark Allen racing Kona, but Peter made becoming an Ironman a reality. I knew if he could do it, I could do it, too.

*

In the spring of 2007, my friend Sarah signed up for her first half-Ironman triathlon and asked me to be part of her support team, along with another Libby Pit dorm alum, Jen Blake, on a weekend-long adventure known as the Wildflower Triathlon at Lake San Antonio in central California. I had raced my first triathlon at Wildflower in 2005, the Olympic distance, but I did not have a wonderful race, and had not raced a triathlon since. I was thrilled to cheer Sarah on, but I did not expect to have another gut-wrenching experience watching the athletes similar to what I felt on the shores of Mirror Lake—but I did. I needed to be a triathlete. I decided on our drive home that I would sign up for an Ironman to race in 2008.

I had set my heart on racing Ironman Wisconsin in September of 2008. However, when I went to the website to sign up for the race, bright and early in September 2007, it was already sold out. It had sold out in only minutes. I was shocked. My heart was broken. I had been thinking of little else but Wisconsin since Wildflower. Now what? I kept searching the website to see if there were any other races in North America around late summer/early fall 2008. "Eureka!" I said as I struck gold (or bourbon maybe). Ironman Louisville was slated for late August, and was open. Perfect. I paid the daunting $500 entrance fee, sat back in my chair and realized I had a little over a year to transform into an Ironman.

Naturally, I went straight to Peter for advice on training. His advice was, "You need to be in the saddle all the time." Got it, I need to ride my bike a lot. Since I had been swimming, riding, and running consistently the last few years, I launched into my Ironman-specific training schedule twelve weeks before the race.

You might wonder how I could have gotten all of that "saddle time" in while working twelve-plus hours a day? The simple answer is that I quit my job. "Whoa, whoa, whoa, what?" Yep, it's true. It was a joint decision between Marion and me that we called our "summer experiment". I would take time off of my job to both train fulltime, and be available for Hannah fulltime. Plus, Marion was working in New Mexico all summer on the movie *Terminator Salvation,* so when Hannah was with us, she would really be with me. I needed to be available for her and my training, but not much else. I appreciated the opportunity to put in the necessary time and energy required to train for my Ironman, but my choice raised the stakes. I didn't want to just finish the race — I wanted to compete.

Training for the race was amazing. I was doing at least two workouts per day for twelve weeks (a crude-but-sufficient training plan that is comical in retrospect), but I made it to Louisville confident and excited to race. The swim was chaotic from the moment I jumped off the pier into the warm, beige-hued Ohio River until I clawed my way to the ladder at the Swim Out section. I ran toward the transition area with jumbled equilibrium, a common result of being horizontal for well over an hour. I am not a great swimmer. Peter popped out of Mirror Lake more than twenty minutes sooner than I did from the river, but I was thrilled that I had met my goal time (1:24) and was finally out of the water and ready to crush myself on the bike.

Oh, the bike...I know that I go on and on about my love for running, and yes I do believe that I am a respectable runner, but riding a bike is really my strong suit. It could have something to do with the fact that my legs make up nearly 80% of my body, and never give me any smart-alecky back talk, and just follow through with whatever I ask them to do. Or it could be because riding a bike is pure fun. It may seem strange that the bike portion of an Ironman is the fastest part of the day for me, because it usually takes about six hours to complete, but that time goes by in a flash. It could be the fact that the course and equipment require 100% attention; there is no time to daydream. A sharp corner needs to be slowed down for, and a tire could pop instantly, plus the entire goal is to push the pedals as hard for as long as possible to gain a better position in the field. I love yelling, "On your left" (the cordial alert when passing other cyclists), and feeling the wind in my face when powering through a long straightaway section, gobbling up men and women on my way to the transition area. In my opinion, riding bikes is fun, hard, and above all, a great way to loosen up the legs for a marathon.

Luckily, I made up a lot of ground on the bike leg from my less-than-stellar swim performance, and was in a great spot to start the marathon. Actually, I had no idea where I was ranked in the race, but I passed many men and women over the 112 miles through the many rolling Kentucky hills, and felt positive that I was at least farther toward the front than I was when I finished the swim.

In case any of you don't remember the distances of an Ironman triathlon, they break down like this: 2.4 mile swim, 112 mile bike ride, 26.2 mile run. This means that when I started my twelfth marathon, I had already been "working out" hard for eight hours in the hot, humid late summer Kentucky sunshine. When I ran out of the transition area, Marion yelled at me, "Now just go run your usual four-hour marathon!" I can't remember if I laughed out loud at him or just to myself. Either way, I thought it was the funniest thing I had ever heard, bless his heart. There was no way in the world I was going to run the marathon anywhere near four hours, but I would certainly try.

The run course consisted of two loops, and was deep with a great crowd along the streets, and top-notch support with aid stations at every mile stocked up with water, wet sponges, hoses, food and flat cola. I chatted with fellow runners along the route, and even though I was not moving very quickly at all, I felt like I was flying. I had never felt so alive. Months of hard work and sacrifice had come down to these precious final moments. I asked one lady how she was feeling around mile eighteen, and she replied, "I just want it to be over! I want to go back to my normal life!"

I chuckled and replied, "I never want this to be over!" She looked at me with a confused, borderline-disgusted expression, but never said a word. I ran ahead of her, and smiled inside and out. I wanted this to be my *new* life, I was at peace with the pain and suffering I endured during training. It felt natural. I craved it, and knew I had found my proper place in the world.

The sun had set at around mile twenty-two, and it was nearly, not quite, but nearly dark when I rounded the last turn toward the finish line set up at 4th Street Live, the epicenter of Louisville nightlife. I crossed the line hearing Marion, my dad, and Hannah cheering for me. Even as I recall that moment, I am tearing up, so I probably was then, too, because it was the greatest experience of my life. The crazy part was that I felt good. Great even. I was smiling from ear to ear: I was an Ironman.

My finish time was 12:52 and change, about an hour faster than my goal time, and my marathon split was 4:28. Not my best marathon time, of course, but a great starting point. I knew I could do better next time.

Marathon #13 – The Long Beach Marathon, 2008

The Battle With LA Traffic

When I returned home from Louisville, my mind was brimming over with ideas about how to become a faster triathlete, and I devoted all of my energy toward that pursuit. However, I could not just sign up for another Ironman in the next few months. For one, there were only a handful of Ironman races in North America, and the upcoming races slated for the fall were all sold out. Also, Ironman races are expensive. The entry fees are pricey, and then there is all of the travel to consider, so I needed to brainstorm and find a local race that would move me in the right direction without bankrupting our household.

I ran my thirteenth marathon in October 12, 2008 in lovely Long Beach, California, again. I think it is fair to admit that I was a wee bit overconfident leading up to this race, which may explain the large dose of karma that dumped on top of me early race morning. I have made it my creed to leave my house no later than two hours before any start time, and since I lived about fifty minutes north of Long Beach, I was safely on the road by 5 a.m. Unfortunately, the traffic gods wagged their fingers at me and my cavalier attitude, and cemented me in traffic.

This sort of scenario is only second to the ultimate nightmare of sleeping through my alarm clock and missing the race altogether, but I was pretty miffed. Let me just say that I have the utmost respect and understanding of the freeway and overall traffic situation/way of life for us Angelenos. I am not an amateur. I spent most of my early twenties in my Honda Civic driving all over Los Angeles while working as a production assistant, and I can tell you that nothing was more valuable to me than my Thomas Guide and upbeat adventurous attitude. I got lost more times than I can count; however, I view getting lost as just an alternative way of finding the desired destination. That said, I guarantee that I could give you seven different options of getting from Point A to Point B in the greater Los Angeles area. The most coveted secret of all: Fountain Avenue in West Hollywood, better known as the freeway of Hollywood. (*You're welcome.*)

Needless to say I make it a habit to give myself *plenty* of buffer time when traveling anywhere in L.A., but that amount of time bloats tremendously on marathon morning. The drive itself from our apartment in North Hollywood to Long Beach was smooth, and curse-word-free, but it took me nearly an hour just to exit the freeway. *Grrr.* After I finally surrendered to my predicament, I said out loud to myself, "Oh well, this is a chipped race," meaning that my official time would start not when the gun went off but when I crossed the starting line and the plastic chip woven through my laces would ping the sensor to let the universe know I was finally on my way.

Once I finally parked successfully and trotted on down to the start area, I hit up the port-o-lets (the most important part of the day), then sprinted across the starting line, carefully weaving my way through the "back of the packers" who were either jogging s-l-o-w-l-y or walking. Suddenly, my killer instinct switched on and I started to dart in and out of the snail-like crowd like an NFL running-back; my usual cool demeanor was still stuck on the 710, and my evil twin, "Terry", had taken me over completely. (My college roommates had nicknamed my belligerent drunken alter ego Terry, because I loathe that name with a passion.)

The course was slightly annoying because it narrowed down from the width of a normal street to a slender concrete bike path along the sand around mile seven. This meant that if I wasn't throwing elbows before, I certainly was now. I think I was running at a respectable pace up until the halfway mark, then my cockiness caught up with me and I started to lose steam.

The most memorable part of this race is the mile twenty-three marker because it is so close to the end, and it sits at the crest of a punchy, sharp hill. So once I saw that sign, I knew I just needed to smile, hit cruise control and enjoy the rest of the ride on in to the finish.

My time was fine. Not amazing, but decent, 3:45. No matter what happens during the Odyssey of a marathon, there is nothing quite as special as crossing the finish line, no matter how many hours and minutes it takes to get there. I started the race with a chip on my shoulder from being nailed by L.A.

traffic, but I recovered, and discovered a higher gear I had yet to hit in previous races, something that was hugely beneficial. I don't think I battered or bloodied anyone in the process, but if I did, my apologies, and I hope you had a great race. Next time, I will leave the house even earlier.

Marathon #14 – Carlsbad, 2009

Sisterhood

Dreamy Carlsbad, California — or as my friend Molly used to call it, "Carlsgood" — is a wonderful place to be. It's also a wonderful place to run around for most of your morning, and that is exactly what I did on January 25, 2009 for my fourteenth marathon.

I arrived in Carlsbad the night before the race and stayed with my sister, Mary, her wonderful husband, Jim, and their adorable dogs, Sawyer and Tyler. Mary is two years older than I am, and a remarkable human being, but we could not possibly be more different. For example, she is a beautiful 5'6" brunette with olive skin and a fashion sense rivaled only by Anna Wintour, while I am a freckly redhead just shy of 5'11" who applies makeup and wears dresses maybe five times a year. Mary and I had some serious battles growing up. One in particular resulted in me laying a strip of masking tape down the center of our bedroom. My mom really loved that. Another involved a bruised cheek, and there have been way too many bruised feelings to count. However, we always set aside our differences for sixty minutes every Thursday night at 8 p.m. to watch *Beverly Hills 90210*. Our brothers thought that show was miraculous to bring peace between us, and it was. Nothing beats quality togetherness like some quality time with the Walshes. Thankfully, after twenty or so years of not liking each other very much, I can easily say that Mary is one of my best friends, and the person on the other end of my crisis hotline. Unlike Tim and Peter, Mary is not a runner, but she is *literally* my greatest cheerleader, and understands my goals, so it meant a lot to have her cheering for me in person for the Carlsbad Marathon.

Race morning was cold, dark and early. For some reason this race felt special. I was not as excited for it during the weeks of training leading up to it, but standing below the starting line in the pitch darkness of a way-too-early start time with thousands of fellow marathoners, I was brimming with adrenaline, and thrilled to start running.

The first ten miles or so of the course travel along the ocean, and since the race started ridiculously early, we were witness to a beautiful sunrise that gave me both a jolt of energy and clarity. I was simply happy to just have the ability to run a marathon, and felt blessed and thankful to be in my shoes at that beautiful moment.

I saw Mary and Jim around mile eleven (a great place for you future spectators to watch from, because it is far enough into the race to give the runners the pep we need to feel good about how far we have come, and enough zing to keep us trudging through the tough mid-race miles in our near future). Mary was wearing a big sweatshirt, clanging a bell, and screaming her head off. It was perfect. I was both laughing and crying because it was amazing to hear her scream my name in such a positive tone. She did look a little tired — it was about 8 a.m. — so I appreciated her efforts to rise, shine and run with me. Yes, Mary Kelly Heim was actually running next to me for a good minute or so — it was epic!

I have always wanted Mary to be proud of me, even when she thought I was a disgusting troll of a little sister always getting in her way throughout our formative years, and literally making her sick to her stomach because I smelled like baby oil and coconut, apparently. Her sudden desperate display of running to keep up with me that morning granted my wish of over thirty years: my big sister was proud of me.

The next few miles were warm, as I was on pace and felt good. Then I hit a wall just before mile nineteen. There was a turnaround point right at the crest of a short, steep hill, and it knocked me down mentally. Luckily, there was a loud crowd chanting my name at this difficult spot on the course. Powered by the positivity of my new friends' roars, I rounded the top of the hill and careened down the other side to run the final seven miles toward the finish.

My pace had a slowed a bit after battling fatigue at mile nineteen, which is natural so deep into a marathon, but I was still cranking out some quick miles, and just held on as long as I could. I was stunned when just before the final left turn into the finish chute I saw the 3:40 pacer right behind me. That meant I was close to my personal record, and might even qualify for Boston again! I sprinted toward the finish line, high on pride and satisfaction that all of my consistent work to be a pro-triathlete was transforming me into a faster runner. My mind was spinning with thoughts of grandeur about what to do next. I wanted to conquer all of it, and finally felt invincible again.

Marathon #15 – The Palos Verdes Marathon, 2009

Round 2

On May 2, 2009, I once again lined up at Point Fermin Park in San Pedro to give the roads and hills of Palos Verdes my all. The runner turnout was small that year because the Los Angeles Marathon was being held over Memorial Day instead of the typical March date, so my guess is that most runners were saving their legs for the premier Los Angeles basin marathon later in the month. Personally, I love every opportunity I have to run in Palos Verdes, especially if there was a marathon attached, so I did not want to miss it. I am glad I ran the race that year because they stopped putting on the *full* marathon a couple years later – tragic but true. I was confident in my fitness, but the course is difficult and would beat me up no matter whether I was at my best or worst. I looked forward to the challenge.

The day started off on a bright note because I snagged a sweet parking spot close to the starting line, a priceless feat at both the beginning and the end of race day. It was cold, and I was nervous. Not because I was going to run a marathon, but because I was going to run a hard marathon. I sat in my car longer than usual due to my parking luck, listening to music and watching other runners walk down the sidewalk toward the starting line. I guessed most of them were running the half-marathon because they looked cheerful with their broad smiles and cheerful pre-dawn banter. I shook my head with disappointment, muttering, "Weak fools, run the full race." My snide attitude came from lurking envy. Those runners were geniuses to be only running half this brutal course. I was the fool for taking on the full, but I wouldn't be able to live with myself any other way. This course is the real deal: scenic and tough. The starting line was wide and thick with runners, mainly half-marathoners, but everyone is equally naive at the start. The fact remained that any distance on this course would bring us to our knees.

I ripped through the first two miles at around eight minutes each, a nearly red-line pace for me. Then the road went right and up. I slowed down out of necessity and strategy; I had run this hill many times during training and at my first Palos Verdes Marathon in 2004, so I did not let its sudden presence dampen my mood. I was prepared, but it was still painful. Once I crested the two-mile hill I took a sharp left turn which led to a heavenly downhill section that led into miles of flat straightaway. I was ecstatic once I made that left onto Palos Verdes Drive because the toughest part of the race was over. I was relieved, and thrilled with how good I felt, and rewarded myself by picking up my pace and placing internal bets on how long I could make it last. "Hang onto this pace until mile seventeen, Taryn. You look great." On the other hand, "This is a marathon, girl. Remember that." I drowned out the voices and enjoyed running fast, and feeling good.

At around mile ten, I settled in right behind a young lad with an impressive white boy 'fro who was cruisin' at an aggressive pace. Usually, I try to never waste precious time or breath making friends on the race course, but we were in the middle of no-man's land, the race was very sparse with volunteers, and honestly, I just couldn't shake him. It was his first marathon, and he was a fast-paced ball of nerves. Since I was not looking for a personal best, I broke my rule, and kept him company for as long as I could hang with his rippin', I-have-no-idea-how-to-pace-a-marathon, fleet-footed teenage pace. I shared some wisdom along our many miles running side by side, urging him to slow down his pace, but he dropped me at mile twenty. I was happy to see him go ahead; my young apprentice was ready to run his own race. Meanwhile, I could finally relax and suffer in solitude.

I was alone for most of the last 10K. I knew that I was pretty far up in place for the women, but I was not exactly sure where my rank really was, because the course was nearly deserted. The majority of the runners at the starting line were running the half-marathon. They had probably finished hours before and were home gulping beers and giving each other cheers, while us *full* marathoners were chugging along the final miles in lonesome, painful silence.

The course lived up to my expectations and punished my limbs like I knew it would. I did not feel spectacular; I just wanted it to be over. Luckily, the steep uphill at mile two was a welcomed downhill trance-basher at mile twenty-four. As a bonus, the last mile traveled right past the first house my dad had moved into when my parents separated in the mid-'80s. My favorite memories in that house are of playing two-touch football games in the front yard with my dad, Tim, Peter and Mary every Sunday afternoon before we drove back to my mom's house. There was one touchdown pass that my dad threw and I caught, that could have made ESPN's top ten plays of the week. It was impressive, and won us the game. I loved those football games, but loathed Sundays. There is nothing as bittersweet and crushing than starting your day with one parent and ending it with another. I gave the house a quick nod as I passed it just before mile twenty-five, then picked up my pace to leave it behind me.

The last half-mile was my favorite part of the course because after making a wide right turn, the road straightened out and I could finally see the finish line. The crowds were sparse and uninterested, so after I crossed the finish line, I sauntered off to find a tree where I could rest my legs, close my eyes, and swim in the giddiness of another marathon finish. It was confirmed later in the day that I was the third overall female in the race. That was wonderful, but a finish that high up with a time of 3:45 meant that there were not many contenders. Still, I was satisfied to be on the podium for such a challenging race.

Marathon #16 – Vineman, 2009

Stepping It Up

The late spring and early summer months after the marathon in Palos Verdes were filled with a heaping amount of swimming, biking and running as I was set to race Vineman, a grassroots "iron" distance triathlon in the gorgeous wine country of Sonoma County. (I can't refer to the race as an Ironman, because Ironman is a brand, but the distance is the same.) I was nervous if my preparation for Vineman was as sufficient as it was for Louisville, but this time I had experience under my belt, and was thrilled to take a crack at another 140.6 mile triathlon.

Sonoma County is in northern California, a good seven-hour drive from my house; still, I considered it a "local" race because it lies within the boundaries of the Golden State, a rarity for long-distance triathlons. Therefore, even with the long drive, I felt like the *hometown* girl. We rented a house for a week along the Russian River for the whole Spates family to descend upon and attempt our first *real family* vacation. Well, it would be a vacation for Marion and Hannah, and a "work" week for me, I guess, but it was wonderful nonetheless. The house had a deck right above the river, which was excellent for father/daughter fishing, and early morning swims for me.

Another reason I chose to race Vineman was because of its prime proximity to my extended family who live in the Bay Area. I was lucky enough to have a full roster of folks planning to attend: two sets of parents, two sets of aunts and uncles, my stepsister Sarah, Peter and his family, Hannah's cousin, plus my original support team, Marion and Hannah. It was a mini-reunion that I was ecstatic to be responsible for, and giddy to reap the benefits from.

Peter drove the hour-long drive north from his office in San Francisco on the Friday night before the race to both calm my nerves, and pump me up. Also, he wanted to be there bright and early to watch the swim. He knew the swim was my weak link, and gave me tons of tips to get me prepped for the 2.4 mile, two-loop course up and down the Russian River, but it was up to me to put my training to the test once my goggles were on and the gun went off.

The first loop was a blur, except for the bridge we swam under which I made sure to note on my second loop as a marker that it was nearly over. When I leaped to my feet to run toward the transition area, I saw Peter cheering for me, "Way to go, Tar!" Then I caught a glance at the clock: 1:14, *What?!* I was shocked and thrilled because that was ten minutes faster than I had swum in Louisville. Success! Next, a volunteer ripped off my wetsuit, which felt both violating and helpful. I thanked him with a wide faster-than-last-year swimmer smile, and quickly mounted my bike and pedaled as fast as I could.

The early morning fog lingered for the first couple of hours of the ride, but the vineyards along the course were breathtaking and broke through the fog with their endless emerald green vines of nature's decadence. Unfortunately, those same vineyard roads were bumpy, and not closed off to traffic, which made dodging cars another obstacle to contend with. However, I was excited to see a familiar gold Jeep Cherokee peel off the road up ahead about twenty miles in and watch four harried adults pour out, yelling and screaming for *me*! The four Jeep bandits were my mom, stepdad, Kent, and Alexa's parents, Penny and Ian. They were jumping up and down yelling my name; it was hysterical. Then as quickly as I passed them, they careened by me again and pulled off to do the same cheering Chinese fire drill. They repeated this about three times before I made a left on the course, which led into the technical portion of the course that thankfully they decided not to explore. It was wonderful to see them when I did; they gave me a bolt of energy and humor I desperately needed to keep pedaling the many muscle-mangling miles ahead.

I rolled into the transition area from the 112-mile bike portion of the race both naive and excited about the marathon. I had not explored the run course during the days before the race, so I had no idea what was ahead of me. I had my time from Ironman Louisville to hit or dip below. I had already slashed a lot of time on the bike course from my time in Louisville, so the run started stress-free. Except for the lead logs below my waist, I felt awesome.

The course traveled up and around the farmland and

vineyards of Windsor, California. Many local families lined the streets, along with their horses and cows, to cheer us on. The course was blanketed with trees along the difficult hilly sections, and wide open to sunshine during the character-building straightaway section leading up to the turnaround point. I had no idea where I ranked among the masses that were trotting along with me, but I felt good considering it was 2:30 in the afternoon and I was just starting out on the marathon.

I noticed many men and not very many women on the course, which is the annoying trend for triathlon. Come on ladies, let's rally and build up our numbers! My pace was not swift, but it was steady, which I thought was more valuable considering this was only my second long-distance triathlon. I still had mountains of experience ahead of me to climb.

For example, the feel of a stand-alone marathon versus a marathon within an ironman is day-and-night different. I learned that lesson really quickly. Nevertheless, I was happy with how my body held up strongly throughout the whole day. After over seven hours of swimming and biking I could still hold myself together to run a 4:12 marathon, an eighteen-minute improvement from my time in Louisville. That excellent marathon time, coupled with my faster swim and bike splits, sliced off forty-four minutes from my overall time. It was a commendable improvement from Ironman Louisville, and I was on top of the world.

I cherish this race because it was the end of my innocence as a triathlete. After I crossed the finish line, I was flooded with delusional dreams of becoming one of the elite. My family did not aid in bringing me down to earth at all. They were so proud of me, and boosted my ego toward the heavens. We all celebrated an evening of pure bliss back at our rental house on the river, fueled by pizza, beer and ice cream.

Marion, Hannah, our dogs and I loaded up in our truck and headed south the following Monday. It was a lovely, but gnawing eight-hour drive down the coast as I plotted my next race and training plans. I had crossed over from spirited athlete to obsessed goal-setter. All I could think about was what I needed to do to qualify for Kona, the Ironman World Championships. What race I should sign up for? How much I should train? Luckily, Hannah slept through my crazed jabberings most of the trip. But Marion listened and just lent fuel to fire, professing that there was no reason I could not become a pro, in fact, there should be no excuse why I shouldn't. He challenged me to go for it. I sat for hours staring out the window watching my gorgeous state stream by at 70 mph, dreaming about the road ahead.

Taryn Spates

Marathon #17 – The Long Beach Marathon, 2009

Still Learning

Ugh. My 17th marathon was run in Long Beach again, for the third time, and it was not pretty. I signed up for Long Beach again because I was ravenous for all things "becoming a professional triathlete." I had no idea what I was doing, but I figured racing another marathon was a good bet to help my cause.

I started the race off at a quick pace with my fellow quasi-speedsters. I did not have to pinball around like I did on my last go-around on this course, because I left my house earlier. However, I assumed I would be faster than a lot of my fellow runners because of the two Ironmans I had in the can. But I wanted too much too soon, and this race was a wake-up call.

The first seven to eight miles were quick and fun. I felt springy on my toes and confident in my experience. Then my stomach cramped and gurgled just before passing mile ten. I stopped for a few minutes to gather myself and hopefully alleviate the situation, but that needful respite threw my pace and psyche into a tailspin. I was upset with my body's uncooperativeness, and I did not regain my focus and resolve until the crowd thinned out around mile twelve. Thankfully, I doused my head and face with water at the mile fourteen aid station, a miracle reprieve. It relaxed every muscle and raw emotion, which meant I could get down to business and run my own race.

The crowd support is top notch along the streets of Long Beach in early October. I can never get enough of the *Rocky* anthem blaring out of speakers perched on every other driveway. Unfortunately, my mind started to wane and energy deplete around mile sixteen, just before we entered the Cal State Long Beach campus. I was exasperated and annoyed because I wanted to get myself together to look good in front of the co-eds. For some ludicrous reason, I felt like I was still one of them. Thankfully, those kids did the trick. My ego took over and my cadence quickened after mile seventeen. I felt like myself again and started to pick off a few runners as we ran outside of the campus. Then I cracked again. Once I cleared mile twenty, I could not feel my legs.

My pace was not impressive, but I still felt like I could hold on and finish fairly strong. Not a personal record, but respectable. Nope. I carried on through each aid station the last six miles, pouring water over my head and into my gullet, slurping down gels, pleading with myself to simply survive to the finish. I was ashamed, and disappointed, but I kept going. Once again I smiled at the mile twenty-three marker because sooner rather than later, this race would be over. I accepted that I was far, far away from where I thought I was when I started this race, and light years away from where I wanted to be. Pro triathletes do not run marathons in over four hours.

I rounded the last left corner down the hill in to the finish chute—one of my all-time favorite finish lines of any marathon, and a definite highlight of this course—but I was bummed to see the clock read 4:09 as I crossed the line. I walked swiftly through the recovery area, frustrated and upset, but as I looked back toward the people still running in (lots of people), I realized I should be proud. I had just run my seventeenth marathon, for goodness' sake! Instantly, I decided, "Today I celebrate, tomorrow I plan."

Taryn Spates

Marathon #18 – The Santa Barbara Marathon, 2009

A Stepmother's Remorse

In early December 2009, only two short months after the Long Beach Marathon, I toed the line at the inaugural marathon in Santa Barbara, California. I was excited about the race because I love that area of our Golden State; it is scenic, rich in history, adjacent to the ocean, and just a two-hour drive north from my house. I went into it with the mindset of "just enjoy the day," because anything would be better than Long Beach. However, as the weekend approached, I felt suffocated by parental guilt. I would have to flee Hannah's playoff soccer game early that Saturday in order to high-tail it north in time to check in for the race. I made it a mission to hold Hannah as my top priority, but as I was told there was *no race day* check in, I would have to leave her game early in order to run at all.

Hannah's team was average. Chances were they would lose the game, but I was the team parent, and had never missed one of her practices, let alone a game, all season. I felt like I was not only abandoning her, but her fellow players and their parents, too. The entire team looked to me for guidance, and I would be abandoning all of them on the most important game of the season. When the witching hour arrived, I walked off the field with a heavy heart before the whistle blew and drove as fast as the law allowed north to Santa Barbara.

I barely slept at all that night. I spoke with Hannah before I *tried* to go to sleep. She was fine, not mad at me at all, but my guilt formed a tight, uncomfortable lump in my stomach that tormented me most of the night. Her team had lost the game.

I must have slept some slight amount, because soon enough I was awake and sitting on the jolly 4 a.m. bus ride toward the starting line. We were driven straight up the 101 north to an elementary school where they dropped us off and loaded us in to a multi-purpose room to sit and wait for nearly two hours until the 7 a.m. start. I did not mind the cattle-pen-like enclosure because it was freezing outside, and my cold threshold is fragile at best. I chatted up a newbie marathoner who was racing her first marathon. My favorite: fresh meat. I tried my best to both excite and calm her nerves for the big day she had ahead of her. Shortly after our bonding session began, we were both on our feet and stepping outside to get in our last potty stops and stretches before the start.

The sun was gently peeking out above the mountains to our backs when the gun fired and we were off! The pace was fast, too fast, but I went with the flow the first few miles, then settled into a more mortal pace between miles five and six. We were running directly into the sun for the first ten miles, which felt comfy and warm, but blinding. I felt good, and just aimed for a solid, steady race.

All was right with the world until we entered a beautiful

and quaint neighborhood just past mile fifteen. I took in water and electrolytes at the aid station, but I felt lightheaded and somber. Then I slowed to a barely jogging pace to take stock of what was going on. I felt alone, and overwhelmed with guilt that I had left my family behind to come run this marathon *by myself* among thousands of strangers. I questioned my crazed level of selfishness and started to get angry. Suddenly, I heard Marion's voice in my head, screaming at me to, *"Go!"* and make him and Hannah proud, so I picked up my feet from their self-loathing trot and started to run.

The course was breathtaking. A cool breeze cut the Southern California winter morning heat, and I was thrilled to be running through this glorious and historical city. My spirits were still high until I rounded a left hand turn and stared straight into the bottom of a hill which promised a long climb to reach mile twenty four. Brutal. (*A quick note to all you race directors and/or prospective race directors: please do not place the largest hill on your courses at mile 24. It is both cruel and a personal record crusher. Thank you.*)

I pitifully ran up the hill and down the other side to make another left turn along the ocean toward the finish line. Over the last mile, I was surrounded by happy runners and ecstatic spectators, but I drowned out their positivity and only heard the slow thump of my broken heart as I crossed the line in 3:55. The look on my face and posture said it all; I was disappointed and confused with my performance.

While licking my wounds on the drive home back down the coast, and having a soul-saving conversation with Mary, I realized that running stand-alone marathons was not helping me become a stronger triathlete. I decided that Santa Barbara would be my last marathon, and I would shift my concentration solely to training and racing triathlons.

Marathon #19 – Vineman, 2010

All In

On the night of November 22, 2009, I walked out of our office, plopped down on the gold crushed-velvet chair my stepdad lent me years before to help furnish my second "real world" apartment, and said to Marion, "I need to race Arizona." I had spent the better part of my Sunday staring at our computer watching the live coverage of Ironman Arizona. I had cheered for my favorite pros, and stalked my competition in my age group. I realized the top athletes in my age group were not entirely out of reach. I thought that if I was properly trained and tuned up, I could make a strong impression the following year and possibly earn a slot to Kona.

Marion replied, "That's what I've been telling you for months. You can beat those girls. You need to believe in yourself and go do it."

I wanted to spring to action right then, but it was late and I needed to go to bed. Nevertheless, the wheels in my head were turning, and the ultimate year-long plan of action started to take shape.

The following morning, I was ready to pounce when registration opened at Ironman.com and I was able to sign up for Ironman Arizona. This race is one of the most popular on the Ironman circuit and has historically sold out in minutes, so I was thrilled when my application went through, and I was officially registered for the race. My race with destiny was exactly 364 days away. My sole focus was qualifying for Kona; I was willing to do anything.

I filled the remaining weeks of 2009 making key decisions to help give me the best chance possible to be fit and ready to crush Ironman Arizona by November. First, I hired a coach, professional triathlete Hillary Biscay. I chose Hillary because she had years of coaching experience, was a successful pro triathlete, was one of the top swimmers in the pro ranks, and our parents were good friends. In fact, I recognized her last name when I started to geek out on pro triathletes in 2007, but when I found out she was a local girl, she quickly became my favorite pro to root for.

Hillary lived in Tucson, Arizona, which meant we did most of our interaction over email and on a savvy workout database where she posted and kept track of all of my workouts. We did have one kick-off phone call just after I finished the Santa Barbara Marathon, where we discussed my goals for the year, etc. I am positive my voice trembled because I was more than slightly star-struck. Hannah stared at me while sitting on a stool just off the kitchen, shaking her head and whispering, "T-Bear, you're such a dork."

It was true: I was freaked out on the inside. I had been following her career for a couple of years at that point, so I was shocked and amazed that she was fired up to guide me through 2010 and raise me to another level. All I cared about was qualifying for Kona by any means necessary, and I had faith that Hillary was the right choice to help make that happen.

Next, I scoured the internet for deals on a triathlon bike. I was ready to walk the walk with the legit triathletes and purchase a carbon time-trial bike; my road bike clip-on aero bar days were over.

Hillary started me off with a track interval workout on January 1, which was awesome. I felt like I was in high school again. Unfortunately, I did the workout wrong. Oops. I gave myself too much rest in between 400 meter repeats, a rookie mistake I would never make again under Hillary's watch. She wanted to boost my marathon speed a bit, so I raced a few half-marathons during the first part of the year, a half-Ironman, and an Olympic distance triathlon. One of the half-marathons was along the always challenging Palos Verdes course, but it was a real treat because I ran with Tim, my stepsister Jen, and stepbrother Bo. However, it was the Olympic distance triathlon that Bo competed in as well that was a true highlight of the year.

Bo is two years younger than I am, and is Sally's youngest child, so he is the baby of all eight of us kids. He and I have always had a unique bond, which made training and racing with him all that more special. Regretfully, I came down with a nasty cough days before the race, so it was not my best performance, but the time spent training and racing with Bo was priceless. Moreover, Bo had a fantastic race. He swam well—which as he was a nearly professional surfer was not too surprising—but he also crushed the bike and run legs, a solid performance which proved he was a natural triathlete. I enjoyed that race, but learned a lot from it, too. There was much more work to be done.

I had Ironman Arizona on my schedule, but November being so late in the year, I wanted to race during the summer, and I thought Vineman was an excellent choice. Hillary agreed Vineman was a great opportunity to test out the work we had accomplished from the first half of the year. But she did not put too much pressure on me; it would just be a benchmark race. This time around was completely different because, instead of my family joining me, I raced alongside my oldest friend from college, the swimming- and cycling-extraordinaire Sarah, and her two adorable lovey-dovey friends Erin and Matt. It would be their first ironman distance triathlon, my third ironman and nineteenth marathon. It was great to be back in Guernesville. We rented a hip house in the woods and spent the few days leading up to the race driving the course and psyching each other up. But soon enough it was bedtime on Race Day Eve.

Once again Peter rallied up from San Francisco to spend the night, and then shuttled us to the swim start race morning at Johnson's Beach on the Russian River. I was very excited for the swim leg of the race because I had spent *many* hours in the pool the previous seven months. Hillary is a swimming machine, and her carefully designed swim workouts are legendary, so I was excited to test my progress. I felt stronger than usual throughout the swim, but I did have to pause twice in order to adjust my leaky goggles. Still, I assumed my time would improve from the previous year. Nope. Guess what my swim time was? 1:14!!!! The exact same time as in 2009. I couldn't believe it, but I regrouped while stripping off my wetsuit and sorting out my bike gear, and vowed to leave my sore arms and attitude behind and pedal hard throughout the 112-mile bike leg.

The bike leg was awesome—until it wasn't. I pushed hard the first loop of the two-loop course, passing people and smiling. Then at mile 100, tragedy struck. I was at the bottom of the biggest hill on the course, Chalk Hill, and my bike locked as I was shifting to an easier gear prepping for the climb. But I couldn't shift. "What the—?" I walked up to the top of the hill, where I asked a couple of spectators in cycling gear to come check out my bike to see if it was rideable.

"Yeah, you're fine, you just can't change gears," said the tall one in a breezy tone.

I felt the fury of my alter-ego, Terry, creeping in, but once I got the haphazard thumbs-up, I threw my leg over my bike and pedaled down the other side of Chalk Hill as fast as I could. Luckily, I only had about twelve miles to go, but having to push hard with no help of easier gears to rest my legs plundered my performance for the marathon.

When I rolled into transition, I saw my dad and Peter cheering and smiling, but I quickly yelled out in an inflamed temper-tantrum tone, "I had a bike mechanical, and lost ten minutes!" My poor dad. He had flown up solo just to see the race, and he must have been less than thrilled to know my attitude was a few notches below joyful.

I cannot explain what a mental bomb I experienced with my bike issue. It was embarrassing. I needlessly loaded a ton of pressure on my shoulders to race perfectly not only for myself, but to make Hillary proud, and to back up the "seasoned triathlete" propaganda I was preaching to my friends all week. Thankfully, I still had a marathon to run, and we all know how running can bring me back from the brink of self-destruction. So I threw in all my chips, and yelped pitifully, running out of transition, "Let's go, T!"

I will save you all from the gritty details of what went on during the marathon. It was not pretty. To sum up, I made more pit stops than I could count, and after crossing the finish line I literally burst into tears. 'Twas not a shining moment. The upside is that I finished in 11:47, knocking off about thirty minutes from my previous year's performance, placing second in my age group, and completing my nineteenth marathon to boot. Even better was that I had the chance to cheer on my friends to their finishes, and had the most fun post-race day lounge fest ever at our swanky house that following Sunday. Obviously I did not have that much to be upset about, but I had a whole lot to learn from. Ironman Arizona was only four months out.

Marathon #20 – Ironman Arizona

Mother and Daughter Road Trip

As the SoCal air started to cool from late summer to fall, Ironman Arizona was quickly approaching and I was ready to put my year-long focused triathlon training through the final exam. Much of the challenge of Ironman racing is not just about what happens on race day, but also the logistics leading up to the race. It's necessary to arrive a minimum of three days before the race because they do not hold the race expo the Saturday before. I am not sure if this planning by the World Triathlon Corporation (the company that owns the Ironman brand) has to do with the commitments to the host towns to have their athletes staying longer than just two nights, thereby spending more money, or if they just want to allow for proper rest time leading up to the main event. Ideally, I wanted a driving partner just in case any funny business came up. Marion and Hannah had to fly out Saturday night because of work and school, respectively, but we would drive back together that following Monday. "Eureka!" I had an idea for some amazing mother-daughter bonding. I thought this trip would be a wonderful chance for my mom and I to spend some uninterrupted time together, and nothing spells out "quality time" like a road trip in the desert.

My mom is the most beautiful woman I know. Marion is very excited about his future because luckily for both of us, I look a lot like her. However, there is much more to my mother than her gorgeous exterior. She is brilliant, hardworking and an eternal optimist. More importantly, she has been a tremendous role model to both me and Mary of how to harness and utilize the powers of being a single mother. She had to schlep four of her kids all over the planet to zillions of practices, games, meets, cheerleading competitions, etc., for the better part of her adult life, so I figured why not one more sporting event where she could just relax and come along for the ride. Thankfully, she agreed.

After my parents' divorce, my mom went back to college, and became an award-winning high school English teacher. Meanwhile, she was raising four children between the ages of eight and sixteen. I have to admit that I used to find it aggravating when she picked me up from junior high school hours after the bell rang because she had to work. As it became routine, I grew to appreciate my after-school adventures in the library. As a grownup, and parent myself, I finally understood the heroics it took for her to hightail it from work thirty minutes away from my school in order to pick me up before dinner. In turn, I have experienced *many* nail-biting moments racing up the 405 freeway from my old office in Santa Monica to pick up Hannah from daycare in Encino during rush hour traffic. Not fun. I am one lucky girl to have had my mom in my corner through years of intense club soccer teams, broken basketball dreams, and every pep-infused phone call I make before my races. Simply put, my mom is the best.

Since my mom and stepdad live in Claremont—my home town—the drive to pick her up was easy because Claremont sits right on the 10 freeway, the main thoroughfare to Arizona. Throughout the six-plus hour drive, my mom and I talked about current events, my brothers and sisters, and lots of triathlon pro talk. I told her all about Hillary, naturally, and the greatest triathlete of all time, Chrissie Wellington. Chrissie had won the Ironman World Championships in Kona from 2007 to 2009, but she had to bow out on race morning in 2010 because she was incredibly sick. She had vowed to make her comeback at Arizona only eight weeks later. Yes, it was true: I would be racing alongside the *best of the best*.

The following morning when I was in line for packet pick up, my mom was standing just a few feet away waiting for me under a tree, when a sinewy, tan and ripped arm slid in front of me and said to the volunteers in a casual English lilt, "Can I check in quickly? I have to hurry on to the pro panel."

I turned toward my mom, my eyes bugging out of my head, heart pounding through my small-chested chest, and mouthed, "That's Chrissie." She laughed, understanding right away what a *huge* moment that was for me, and told me later in her classic, adorably sentimental voice that seeing Chrissie was a sign of "exciting things ahead" for my race.

I could never convey to my mom how special those two days and nights were for me to spend with her, just the two of us, in Tempe, Arizona before the most significant race of my life. I had not only physically prepared for this Ironman, but I had invested heaping amounts of time, energy, money and both mental and emotional fortitude in pursuit of this singular goal. Having my mom there with me gave me breath in my lungs to enjoy it all.

Let's back up just a smidge. After I raced Vineman for the second time in July, and my swim time did *not* improve at all, Hillary ordered five weeks of "swim camp," which meant hours and hours of swimming every day for five weeks. This daily fun time in the water luckily coincided with Hannah's gymnastics summer camp that was a few miles from a splendid outdoor pool I could swim in while she flipped and cartwheeled herself through another adolescent summer. I know it sounds decadent to be able to train all day long, and it is. But it does still require some masterful time management skills in order to plan my four to five hours of training around a child's summer schedule. I did enjoy my long hours in the pool. I think I got faster, but I would not *really* know until race day in November. I did put in lots and lots of riding and running as well, but it was the swim that I was most nervous and excited about.

When race morning arrived, I was up and out *early*. I had a fantastic conversation with a fellow athlete, and mother of four, in my age group in the transition area. This is usually my favorite time of the day, just a few thousand athletes squirming into our wetsuits and awaiting a whole day of exercise and self-exploration.

We waded together in Tempe Town Lake awaiting the cannon for the start. It was the most beautiful morning I had ever seen: the sky was slowly lighting up, there were spectators everywhere, and I was pumped to put my extensive swim training to the test. The swim is one big loop, which is my favorite because there are only a few turns, which meant less chance of getting mowed down by faster swimmers blazing up behind me on their second loop. I had my fair share of elbows to the head, and knees to the ribs, but I felt amazing. I climbed out of the lake and looked at my watch, 1:12. "*Yes!!*" That was a two-minute personal best, but it felt like twenty minutes. I was so proud that I had executed my swim correctly, and smiled (and shivered) all the way through transition to the change tents.

I started the three-loop bike course confident and ready to unleash the long-legged beast that I had been feeding and coddling for months. It was time for my "bike" legs to show up. Unfortunately, we had a wretched headwind on the way out to the turnaround spot, and the roads were *very* crowded, but we did have a killer tailwind on the way back to town, which was mighty helpful. To add to the excitement, there was a steady stream of rain mixed in for good measure, so even though it was a flat course, it required skill and grit.

I was confident Hillary had prepared me well. I maintained my pace throughout each loop, and drank up the roaring cheers from my family at the turnaround spot in town. Their enthusiasm may have been enhanced by their encampment at a local bar during the five-plus-hour bike leg. They sure were happy to see me. Meanwhile, I kept grinding away with each pedal stroke and before I knew it, I was rolling down to transition, hopping off my bike and asking the volunteers in the change tents, "How many girls have come through so far?"

They were lovely and replied, "Just a couple."

It turned out I was 28th in my age group after the swim, which was a bummer, but then I had moved up to 7th place after the bike. Yay!

I started the run quicker than prescribed by Hillary, about 8:40ish per mile pace, but I knew that I needed to feed on the adrenaline while I had it, so I maintained it for as long as possible. As I rounded the first of three loops on the run course I heard Marion yell out,

"You did the bike in 5:43!"

That was a *huge* personal best for me, and gave me an added pep in my step, but nothing could compare to the ultimate thrill of the day—seeing Hillary cheering for me at mile eight of the run. I had yet to actually meet her in person through the whole year that we had been working together, so to hear and see her rooting for me was astounding. I smiled and hoped that she was proud of me.

As I was finishing up the first of the three loops of the marathon, I heard a motorcycle with a cameraman on the back seat speed around me. Yep, Chrissie Wellington was closing in on her *last* loop of the race and onto a record setting Ironman finish time. I gave her a shout, "Great job!" as she passed me, but she was in the zone. I respected that. Plus, I had to focus on my own race. Nevertheless, I felt honored to be running alongside the greatest triathlete of all time minutes before she made history.

The next sixteen miles or so were a grueling tug of war

with the fading sunlight; I did not want to finish in the dark. However, as I was rounding mile twenty-five, I thought I was flying like a cheetah. Not quite. My pace was about nine-minute miles, maybe more actually; either way, that pace would not have me reach my goal of finishing under eleven hours. Then a delightful thing happened. I looked up to above and said, "Thank you." I accepted that it was almost over, this singular race that held so many expectations. It was nearly a memory. However, I felt relieved more than depressed because I realized my journey was far from over. I had too much to learn, and way too many memories left to create, adventures to conquer, and races to race.

Thankfully, along with this exhaustive state of euphoria came a new focus to finish with strength and class. I rounded the last dark left corner before the brightly lit bleacher-flanked finish line, smiling wide, fists pumping in the air. I crossed the line, and ran into the arms of my very proud coach. It was the perfect ending to the most amazing year of my life.

The next morning I followed my last bit of training from Hillary and rode the stationary bike in the hotel gym to flush out my legs, and gain a bit of perspective about what had happened the day before. I had finished the race in 7th place in my age group in 11:12, which meant no Kona slot for me, but I had earned a thirty-five-minute personal record. Sadly, I could not keep Hillary as my coach because I am simply not *that* much of a baller, but she still checks in on me, has become a true friend, and continues to inspire me every day.

Hillary and me just after crossing the finish line

Marathon #21 – Ironman St. George, 2011

Always Bring Salt Tablets

I decided to race in the 2nd annual Ironman St. George about three days after I arrived home from Arizona. To admit this as a complete "What do I do now?" full-on obsessed panic attack would not be an overstatement. I was feeling incredibly insecure and needed to lock up another race just to be able to breathe again. I have previously mentioned that most Ironman triathlons sell out for the following year the day after the race takes place, hence that was why I was in such a fury to sign up for Arizona so quickly in 2009. This is because the races are both popular and typically only allow 2,500 participants to compete. However, Ironman St. George was scheduled for May 7, 2011, less than six months from when I signed up, and I had no problem getting in… hmmm. I had heard that the course was beautiful, nestled among the red rocks close to Zion National Park, but I had also heard whispers it was extremely challenging. I read more than once, "St. George has the toughest bike/run course combination in North America." Sweet. In any case, I was psyched, still drunk on post-race ambition, and confident that I could carve out a solid training program on my own in less than six months that would have me properly prepped and primed for 140.6 miles in gorgeous St. George, Utah.

The quaint town of St. George is located just a couple hours north of Las Vegas, which made it just over six hours from my house. I set off on my excursion to St. George the Wednesday before the race, because this Ironman would take place on a Saturday rather than the usual Sunday. This schedule change-up was due to accommodate the influential Mormon population in Utah. I planned a pit stop in Claremont to meet up for coffee with my mom and Kent because they would not be able to come to the race due to its being on the same weekend as my nephew Reed's first birthday. Clearly, that celebration took precedence over my 5th Ironman. Nevertheless, it was quite unnerving for my mama to send me off on my own, so this hour or so chatting before my adventure was mutually beneficial for both of us. Fear not! I did have a solid crew of family making the pilgrimage to St. George to support me on race day. My Aunt Corrie and Uncle Fred would be driving over from Arizona, and Marion would be flying in on Saturday afternoon just in time to see me start the run, clutch timing indeed. However, I was on my own for these early days in the red rocks of Utah.

Miraculously, it turned out that I was quickly swallowed up in the fold of a few fellow members of P5, a triathlon club I had joined in the beginning of the year. I was not the most active member of the squad because I lived about forty minutes away from their epicenter, which meant I stuck to my usual solo training. But these folks were great, especially my super-cyclist friend, Mary. They let me tag along with them on their tour of the bike course, a training swim, ride, and an "at home" pro talk with a former professional who shall remain nameless. This is because he/she gave us the most ludicrous nutrition advice that unfortunately I followed on race day...more on that later. Nevertheless, it was wonderful to have the camaraderie of friends in the days and hours before the most daunting physical challenge of my life.

The race day started in pre-dawn darkness with a bus ride from the finish line in downtown St. George out to Sand Hollow Reservoir in nearby Hurricane where we would swim. I loved this kind of bus ride. It reminded me of the airplane flight before skydiving: the only option is to jump.

The swim was absolutely beautiful. My swim fitness was not at the peak it was at Ironman Arizona. I had let that portion of my training slip once I stopped working with Hillary, but I knew I could put in a solid effort and still preserve valuable energy for the difficult bike and run legs that would dominate the day. I was out of the water in 1:16 (*daggonnit!*). However, there was no time to dwell on my lackluster time, because next up was the meat and potatoes of the course, the bike and run.

Let's see, how should I describe the bike course? There are so many adjectives to choose from, but the following are a few adequate examples: hot, steep, windy, challenging, unforgiving, painful, slow, soul-crushing and sad. It was by far the toughest course I had ever pedaled across during an Ironman. Mercifully, my sanity was not completely cracked because the scenery was absolutely stunning. Everywhere my feeble-minded head turned, I was struck with sights of beautiful red rocks, screaming blue sky, and unique late spring desert landscape. It was breathtaking.

The temperatures were in the high 90s, and there was very little shade. I cooked throughout the 6:16 hour ride. It seemed impossible to take in enough fluids, whether water or sports drink, it was never enough. I was about halfway through the ride when I realized I should have taken salt tabs with me, but I had followed the advice from the "pro" I mentioned earlier who had suggested the sodium in the sports drink provided would suffice. Maybe for him/her, but that would not be enough for me. I was losing way too much salt, and salt is needed to prevent an imbalance in electrolytes which could lead to dehydration or hyponatremia. Not good.

On to the *run!* I will sum up the run course with one word: *Wow!* Luckily, I was feeling good when I started the run, and I saw Aunt Corrie, Fred and Marion lined up cheering for me as I exited the transition area, which was heavenly. The course was unreal. The scenery was beautiful, but there was a steaming cloud of dread surrounding every participant. It appeared less like a marathon, and more like a death march. I needed every ounce of expertise to conquer it, but conquer it I did. I refused to let the grueling and incessant hills bring me down. Instead, I embraced the piercing and unrelenting sunlight as an energy source rather than its true identity of Salt-Sucking Sorceress, and never gave in; I ran every step.

The final three miles were shady, and all downhill. The

finish chute was a fabulous slanted section toward the center of town, surrounded by fans and my fantastic mini-yet-mighty crew cheering me on toward my 5th Ironman finish! They must have known this one hurt more than most because I finished in 11:56 — much slower than my recent times — but I had never been so happy at a finish line. After a few minutes of rest, I retrieved my bike and drove back with Marion to the hotel. We planned to all meet up for dinner shortly after we freshened up.

I promise to keep this PG, but it is worth it to keep reading...When I was in the shower, I started to feel faint. I lay down for a minute or two, and proceeded to get sick all over the place. I gained some strength and normalcy when I got dressed and went to my aunt and uncle's room. I told them I wasn't up for dinner, but frankly I had a tough time stringing that simple sentence together. I felt sorry for my Aunt Corrie because she was the only parental figure represented at this race and here I was falling apart right in front of her. She wanted to call an ambulance, but I told her I just wanted to lie down and that I should feel fine later. I could barely make it back to our room, which was only two doors down. In fact, I didn't. I slumped down in the hallway in front of our door and even heard some fellow hotel guests snicker at my "drunk" behavior. But I was not drunk, or dehydrated, but experiencing symptoms of hyponatremia. I had ingested a lot of fluids all day, but lacked enough salt to properly soak them all up. My electrolytes were off balance, hence why I was dizzy, vomiting, and losing consciousness. I was scared.

Once I got inside the room, Marion quickly threw on his

shining armor and forced me to drink two large bottles of water filled with electrolyte tablets, and made me stay awake. All I wanted to do was sleep. Fortunately, I regained my faculties fairly quickly after Marion's magical hydration elixir took hold, and I was able to eat some food that Aunt Corrie brought back to our room from their dinner at the hotel restaurant. Salty French fries were a very wise choice. I felt horrible that she had to see me in that crippled state, especially since I had been the vision of strength, an Ironman, just a few hours earlier. Honestly, I was not at all prepared for what the heat would do to me, and was forced to learn my lesson the hard way. *Always bring salt tabs to an Ironman!*

Marathon #22 – Ironman St. George, 2012

It's not if you go down, but when you go down.

One of my favorite races of all time is the Carpinteria International Distance Triathlon in Carpinteria, California. I first raced it in 2007, my second triathlon ever, then in 2010 with decent results, and again in late September 2011. The city of Carpinteria is about twenty minutes south of Santa Barbara along the gorgeous California coast. It is a small, but lovely race that includes remarkable scenery with challenging terrain that never disappoints. I came into the race in 2011 with fast expectations, mainly because I knew the course and was looking forward to the shorter distance. The three legs break out as follows: 1.5K swim, 40K bike, 10K run—which translates to a fun, fast day at the races.

The swim was a nerve-wracking beach start where we all lined up in our wetsuits and frazzled nerves then sprinted into the ocean when the horn blew. I think I have beaten the "I am not a great swimmer" horse to death by now, so I will save your patience on not reviewing that, but I didn't come out of the water as far ahead as I wanted. There were still a ton of bikes racked in the transition area, though, which was a positive sign. I took off on my bike out of transition and had the confidence of a late '80s Mike Tyson. I was passing tons of people, feeling good and working hard. All was going to plan.

The road was slick because we were in the midst of a heavy dew/constant drizzle that was common for our proximity to the ocean, but not exactly what I was used to coming from my hotbox environment in the San Fernando Valley. I wanted to be smart, and handle my bike correctly while pushing hard in the straightaways and carefully through the curves while maintaining my position in the field. I could smell the podium.

At around mile ten, I shifted gears because there was a sharp right turn ahead that luckily was clearly marked. I slowed down to make the turn, when suddenly, *"Thwack!"* I was down. My shoulder hit the pavement first, absorbing most of the shock. Next, my head slammed hard against the asphalt, the noise causing the greatest alarm. I knew I was hurt. I quickly scrambled up on my feet to get out of the way of passing riders, and shuffled off to the side of the road to assess my injuries. A volunteer in her mid-fifties named Pam was instantly at my side caring for me, and offering to take me to the medical tent at the finish line. Initially, I resisted because I thought I just had some gnarly road rash. But then I glimpsed blood on the inside of my helmet and I took her up on her offer for the ride. Pam was adorable; she kept trying to make me feel better about not finishing the race as we drove back to town. But honestly, I didn't care at all about quitting. I knew my head was hurt, and I had learned at a young age never to fool with a head injury.

When I was in the 4th grade, my sister Mary and I were bullied by a neighborhood thug every day when we walked to and from school. This emotionally mangled pre-teen would do all kinds of disgusting things to us, ranging from hurtful taunting to inappropriate touching with her hands and sticks; it was brutal. My brother Peter was in the 7th grade at the time and he would spend at least an hour with me every day after school, teaching me various fighting techniques to get back at this girl and stand up for myself.

One day in early spring, Mary and I were minding our business walking home and there she was, yelling and grabbing at us, with her nasty younger siblings cheering her on. It was a living nightmare. Suddenly, something switched inside me. I channeled Peter's teachings and backhanded her with all of my might, sending her soaring. I was instantly flooded with the most exhilarating sensation I had ever felt in my life. She literally flew back at least five feet, screamed at us like a whiny toddler, and scurried off to her house with her little brats whimpering behind her. Mary was so proud of me, we high-fived, then bolted home as fast as we could because we were high on our triumph and I wanted to tell Peter about our victory!

Peter was usually home from school when we got home, so we were surprised and let down to find the house completely empty when we came barreling through the front door with our good news. We went about our afternoon business with doing homework and watching *Airwolf* when the phone rang. It was our mom, eerily telling me that Peter had been rushed to the hospital with a head injury. I dropped the phone and burst into tears.

Peter had been swinging in between the two high cabinets in the kitchen, a bad habit my mom warned him daily against, when he had swung too high, lost his grip, and fell to the ground directly on top of his head. My mom was usually in class at that time of day, but miraculously, she was home, and was able to get him the medical care he needed. She told us later that when he fell, it sounded like furniture crashing to the ground. But it wasn't furniture, it was Peter. It gives me chills thinking about what Mary and I would have done if we had found him bleeding on the floor all by ourselves.

The next twenty-four hours were frightening because of the severity of Peter's concussion. He had to be strapped down to the gurney because he started to seize and was swinging his arms all over the place, nearly clobbering his helpful medical team. He was admitted into the ICU for a couple of days, where he was allowed visitors. I remember seeing him weak and drugged up on the bed with tubes plugged in all over his body; it was awful. Thankfully, he made it out okay and was soon classic, goofy Peter again. Naturally, I did not tell him about my glorious smackdown until he was out of the woods. But when I finally did, he was thrilled and extremely proud of me. Moreover, Mary and I never heard a peep out of that bully ever again.

I knew that head injuries weren't anything to fool around with so I was willing for my Guardian Angel Pam to get me checked out. She dropped me off about a block from the med tent because the streets were blocked off to traffic for the race. I thanked her, unloaded my bike and started to walk toward the tent when a man with a stroller ran up to me to help with my bike. It turned out he was a nurse in the Navy. He said I didn't look so good, and he thought I might pass out, which explained his eagerness to help me. He sat me down on a cot in the med tent where I sat alone for a few quiet minutes while my dashing new friend went to find help.

Suddenly, I was on my back, and in a neck brace. Paramedics and firemen were looking over me, asking me all kinds of questions, and prepping to load me in the ambulance to drive to the hospital. I was very hesitant about the necessity of the ambulance, because I thought I was fine, and I knew it would cost a fortune that our insurance would not cover. But before I could protest too much, Marion shouted from the back corner of the tent, "It's okay, Taryn, don't worry about the money. You need to go to the hospital." I had never been so happy to have him with me at a race. The next thing I knew, I was moved onto a gurney and loaded into the back of the ambulance. This frenetic scene unfolded while people were crossing the finish line in front of me; I was beyond embarrassed to be ending the race like this. To add insult to injury, they did not even turn on the sirens for our drive to the hospital, which I silently hoped would mean a savings on our bill.

I was in the emergency room for a couple of hours, where I received x-rays for my shoulders, pelvis and hips. All were fine—once again my *big-boned* body came in handy—but I did need a few staples for a two-inch gash on my head. I was ordered not to swim or run until the staples were removed ten days later. I could pedal on my bike on my indoor trainer, which I did, but it was not nearly enough to maintain much fitness. I was scheduled to run the Malibu Marathon that following November, but I had missed too much valuable training time with my recovery, so I bailed on that race and most everything else. I started to question what on earth I was doing—or not doing—with my life. And I searched for a reason to keep going with my training, and with life in general.

The beginning of 2012 was abysmal at best. Marion was working 100-plus-hour weeks; I am not exaggerating. He had two days off in January: the 1st and the Saturday after his birthday. We are both used to the "indentured servitude" way of life in the visual effects industry, but this stint tested our patience. Therefore, once he was unshackled from his latest project, we jumped at the opportunity to escape L.A. for a few days. Along with our two dogs, Guinness and Marzen, we drove up the coast to a gorgeous campground above Santa Barbara called Lake Cachuma.

I was happy to be having some quality time together, but I was incredibly anxious from the moment we left the house. I could not sleep the first night. I felt trapped by both the wooden walls of the cabin and my own skin. I loved Marion more than anything, but I could not believe what my life had become. I felt that my identity was purely about taking care of Hannah and being supportive of his career. Along the way, I had failed to realize my own dreams of becoming a professional triathlete. I had made my own choices, and I am proud of every one of them, but I had lost the Taryn my high school classmates had voted as student body president, and I feared she might be gone for good if I did not act fast and make needful changes.

I went for a run then next morning in an attempt to shake away my anxiety. The campsite was off a busy highway, so I just ran around the perimeter of the campsite, which was fine, but confining. Marion spent much of the first day searching for a fishing spot. He found a good one, but not many fish. I enjoyed every minute we spent together, but I was still not myself, and felt angry that I was cheating Marion out of his much-deserved vacation.

The second morning of our trip, Marion wanted to go fishing early, which meant that I had to stay with the dogs in the cabin until he got back, and subsequently could not run. Both of our dogs, especially our boy Marzen, were in rare form; he was barking and pacing the cabin, and I could not figure out how to make him calm down. Suddenly, I cracked. I grabbed my notebook and wrote down a manifesto of how my life was a complete failure. I scribbled furiously about how I had no idea who I was anymore, and I did not want to go on one more second. At that moment, Marion walked through the door.

Poor guy. I was a wet, crying mess sitting on the couch, while our dogs were howling and pacing like caged hyenas. He knelt down next to the dogs, pleaded with me to calm down, and then took them outside to see if they had to go to the bathroom. His instincts were right; Marzen just needed a good poop to bring him back down to earth. Unfortunately, I was still in hysterics when the three of them walked back into the cabin. Marion sat next to me and listened to all I had to say, even though much of it must have hurt his ears. He told me I could do whatever I wanted, but I had no idea what that would be.

After what felt like an eternity of dangling off the edge, I decided to go for a run. Marion applauded that idea; clearly, I needed some fresh air. The run was windy, dusty, and not fun at all, but it woke me up. I realized the key to my happiness was running. It was the one part of my life that I owned, had complete control over, and could depend on to give me clarity. I spent the rest of the afternoon cooking up a plan that would give me purpose, while still being able to carry out my every day responsibilities for Marion and Hannah.

The final morning of our "relaxing" vacation, was my first real trail run around Lake Cachuma. It was beautiful, if a little scary because I was not too sure where I was going. But the air was still, my mind was clear, and my legs were ready to carry me. During the run I had an epiphany. I vowed to run thirty-five marathons by the time I turned thirty-five. I was thirty-two at the time, I had twenty-one marathons under my belt, and therefore I needed to run fourteen more within thirty months to reach my goal. I knew I could do it. I would do it. I just needed to figure out how to do it.

I told Marion about my plan to run 35 by 35 and write a book about it all two minutes after we pulled out of the Lake Cachuma campsite. He never flinched, "Okay, get going." I stared out the window, calm and motivated. I knew this quest was right. The true Taryn was back.

I grew up encountering a handful of windy storms that wreaked havoc in Southern California because we are not used to—my mind is blanking, what is it called? Oh right, weather. I always found running and riding in windy conditions incredibly annoying, but not scary. That changed on May 5, 2012 soon after I hopped in the water of Sand Hollow Reservoir for a second go-around at Ironman St. George.

The water was glassy and gorgeous for the 7 a.m. start, near perfect conditions for a 2.4 mile swim with a thousand or so of my nearest and dearest masochistic pals. We were a smiley, happy bunch of overly muscled misfits, swimming into another amazing all-day triathlon.

Unexpectedly, less than ten minutes into the swim, our smiles switched to screams, and our race turned from a feat of endurance to one of pure survival.

The swells grew and began to roll like ocean waves after our first left turn at the buoy. I thought the swell was from the wake of the rescue boats staged in the reservoir, but after the second left turn I realized it was from a massive windstorm that had descended upon us. The race was too far along for the officials to stop it; the only choice was to keep moving toward the finish. I kept my composure because my swim fitness was sufficient, but more importantly I had my childhood foundation of battling waves at Torrance Beach to depend on. Nevertheless, it was futile to attempt any consistent freestyle swim stroke. I was practically body-surfing. I could see the scattered crowd of spectators to my left, hoping Marion and my family held faith that I would make it out of this okay.

After many more minutes than usual, I resurfaced and ran into the changing tents in the transition area, shivering, freezing, but thankful I had made it out of the water alive. I accepted the reality that the expectations I had set for myself for the day were blown away by the 40 mph winds, and my goal shifted from "gain a personal best" to "finish the race in one piece."

I hopped on my bike and rode out of the swim transition, yelling to my family, "Mission aborted!!" I knew the wind was going to continue slamming us on the bike—my swim was twenty-five minutes longer than usual, and I wanted to let them know that this was going to be a much longer day for all of us than we anticipated.

The bike leg was hysterical. Imagine riding your bike as hard as you can into a relentless headwind for nearly eight hours. Thankfully, I had experience on my side. I was not surprised by any portion of the course because I had ridden it the previous year, and it was just as tough as I remembered. Ironically, the steepest hill on the course, "The Wall," turned out to be the easiest part of the day. I had to give a wink and a smile to the heavens as the wind downshifted to a slight breeze after the first sharp right turn up "The Wall." It felt more like a hand on my back than a tornado in my face.

The saving grace of the grueling bike course is its pretty face. There is nothing more glorious in my opinion than the red rocks surrounding St. George, Utah. I was alone for a large portion of the day, but I still felt giddy and appreciative at how hard this race was turning out to be. I knew I was part of something special. Did I think the bike course would never end? Yes. Was I happy with my bike split of 7:27, over an hour slower than my time in 2011? No, but I finished under the cutoff which, considering the conditions, was respectable.

As I rolled into the bike transition area, I had no idea how many athletes did not make the bike cutoff. There was a nervous energy among the athletes, volunteers and spectators. I didn't care. I knew this marathon would take me to another level. I was already beaten to a pulp, and I prayed to simply finish it.

The upside to the 2012 race was that the run course had been moved from the exposed, hot, hilly suffer-fest I ran in 2011 to a much more manageable course that looped around downtown St. George. Even though I appreciated the race organizers' efforts to make our lives somewhat more pleasant, I don't think I had ever been so annoyed during a marathon as I was that Cinco De Mayo in 2012. It was probably because I had never started a marathon so late in the day, around 4 p.m., and my legs and spirit were pretty beaten down by the tormenting winds that had ravaged my soul since sunrise. Miraculously, the air was still for the marathon, another gift from above. Nevertheless, my legs were like cinder blocks, and my stomach was rock hard. After battling all day, it gave out around hour twelve, which I understood; I was usually done by then. I visited a port-o-let and let go of everything I had.

A dark cloud of shame and exhaustion hovered over me between miles ten and twenty. I was sick with self-pity. I am positive the only reason I did not walk off the course and weep in my Spandex™ on the driveway of some well-meaning Mormon's house was that I knew my family was waiting for me at the finish line. I picked up my sorry spirits and ran for them. I knew I would be fine if I quit; I was that delusional. But I didn't quit.

I finished the race in the dark, a sign I had been out on the course too long. Still, I knew I made my family's day when they saw me finish. I could only imagine how worried they had been all day. Apparently, my dad and Marion had spent a lot of one-on-one time together, and even had had rocks thrown at them while driving to a bar. Thanks, St. George!

When we arrived back at the hotel, I stopped in the parking lot to talk to a family who congratulated me on finishing the race. A normal sentiment, yes, but their tone was weighted and sincere because their daughter had not finished. It turned out that Ironman St. George 2012 had the largest attrition percentage ever for an Ironman: 29% of the participants did not finish. That is a *huge* number.

My time was a disappointing 13:39, nearly two-and-a-half hours slower than my best time at Ironman Arizona, but I still had a finishing medal dangling around my neck, and a story to tell. I was proud to be a part of such a historically difficult race, and to have officially kicked off my 35 by 35 quest. Marathon twenty-two was in the books, and I was well on my way to thirty-five.

Marathon #23 – Ironman Louisville, 2012

Back To Kentucky

The summer of 2012 was equally exciting and excruciating. I was training for another Ironman and blazing a course to complete my 35 by 35 quest. Marion started a fantastic new job on the movie *White House Down* where he was asked to help supervise both the shoot of the movie and much of the visual effects work in post-production. I was thrilled for him because it was a huge leap forward in his career, but we were both ill-prepared for the pain and strain the job would put on our marriage, because the shoot was going to take place in Montreal, Canada.

I am well aware that many other spouses endure long stretches of time apart due to military tours of duty, and other jobs that take place in the film industry. I am proud of and impressed by all of them who can make it through just fine, but I am not one of those people. I was depressed, sad, and angry for most of the four months Marion was in Montreal. Luckily, I had my training, Hannah, and my dogs to keep me focused and moving forward.

The one day I needed something more than my run, my miracle was our dog Marzen. I was sobbing during my run, once again sad about Marion being gone and feeling like I was wasting my life doing nothing at all but working out and waiting for him to come home. But Marzen needed me. He needed me to bring him home from a long night alone at the vet's office after a teeth cleaning, and to hug him, kiss him, and love him the rest of the afternoon. When I saw him walk out from the holding area after his surgery he was so happy to see me. I was everything to him at that moment, and he was everything to me. My boy Marzen rescued me that day by letting me rescue him. He made me whole again, and gave me the confidence to keep my training up in order to be as fit as possible when I headed back to Louisville for the Ironman in late August.

Once again, Louisville was a special place to race. This race was a little different than the first time I competed in 2008, because I did not have anyone from my family along to support me. Marion couldn't get away from work, and it was a little far for my parents to come out a second time. However, I did have a few friends racing, which made the final prep days leading up to the race fun because I shared them with people I respected and cared about. To be honest, it was nice to not worry about keeping anyone entertained, plus I always enjoy a little quality "T Time," and I knew everyone would be tuning in online, so I still felt the love even if it was from afar.

When Sunday morning rolled around I was ready to race. The morning was warm and pleasant, but the swim line was *L to the O to the N to the G!!! LONG!!* This swim is unique because they have a time trial start, which means we all wait in line to jump off the pier into the river one by one. Still, I was in the water by about 7:25, and rocking my new TYR Torque, a swim-skin speed suit which did not have the amazing buoyancy powers of my wetsuit, but was helpful nonetheless. I felt pretty good while swimming past Toe Island, but once we made the turn, I slipped out of my rhythm. My swim stroke had vastly improved this year, and since the St. George swim had been more like a squall than an Ironman swim, I was looking forward to seeing how my improved form would translate in Louisville. Sadly, when I finally allowed myself to look at my watch while climbing up the stairs of the swim exit, I felt sucker-punched. I saw the digits 1:20. *"What the F%^*?!!"* I knew it was not a fast swim, but I was hoping for a 1:10, so I just pictured my day *blown!* This deflation in spirit explains why my transition time was an eternity. After a few minutes of whining and whimpering I put the swim behind me, and pedaled off to go crush it on the bike.

As soon as I started pedaling, I felt like I had all the energy in the world, and got to work right away on River Road. The first ninety miles of the bike were an absolute dream. I was pushing hard the entire way and just had to giggle to myself at how much easier this course was compared to St. George. However, a little bit of St. George came back to haunt me around mile ninety in the form of a nagging headwind that slowed me down. I was working towards a 5:40 split, but the last fifteen miles blew that out the window. I didn't let that disappointment overwhelm me like the swim had, because I needed to take into account saving my legs a bit for the marathon. I decided to play it smart and just keep a quick cadence to spin out my legs, get in at a decent time, and move on to the run.

I was a happy camper when I ran into the transition area. It could be because there were not many women in the tent (always a good sign), but also because running always brings me out of a funk and my day had been pretty funky thus far. I just wanted to go run, and luckily I had 26.2 illustrious miles waiting for me.

This was my twenty-third marathon, and even though I am still fairly new at Ironmans, I feel pretty confident at running marathons, and I executed this one almost perfectly. My first thought was to stay conservative for the first ten miles, which I wanted to do for my mother (I knew she was worrying). I did not want to push it too hard, too early. I was methodical about what I would eat and drink at each aid station, and just maintain my pace, which I thought was a four-hour pace, although my math was off. Fortunately, I did not discover my mistake until mile twelve. At that point I was pretty bummed, because it was more like a 4:20 pace, but then I was just thankful that I had been ignorant up until that point, and kept clicking off the miles.

Oddly enough, I did have a surprising sensation overwhelm me around mile fourteen that I had never felt in a race before: sleepiness. I blame the mere three hours of restless sleep I had gained the night before or perhaps it was the gallons of sunscreen that had flooded my eyeballs all day. In any case, I just wanted to curl up on the sidewalk and take a nap. Obviously, that did not happen. Instead, I adjusted my aid station plan and decided to start drinking cola earlier than usual; I was holding out to start drinking it at mile twenty, but I started at sixteen instead. Immediately the sugar and caffeine from the cola took hold, and I woke up and was back on pace.

I am not sure if I have ever shared this with anyone but Marion—he thinks it's weird—but whenever I feel in an amazing running groove, I feel really tall. And from mile seventeen on, I felt like a giant. I took advantage of how amazing my body felt because I knew that this surge might not last long. However, I just kept feeling stronger and stronger as the miles clicked by, and I knew I was taking minutes off of my pace—*yay!*

My original goal for the day was a sub eleven-hour finish. That was not to be, but I did see a possible sub-11:40 in my future, and my bod did not let me down. I pushed the last couple of miles, and ran that final half-mile like the end of a cross country race, fast! I probably could have spread that speed out across the entire marathon, but I thought I executed it well because my first eighteen miles were controlled, which set up the last eight miles to be the fastest of the day. I finished the race in 11:36, a full two hours faster than my finish time at St. George.

I was thrilled because I had finished another Ironman, always a difficult feat, and this time with no family members to hug me or fetch me water after the race. I did it on my own. Also, I was able to support my friends as they finished a few hours later. I had never walked back to the finish line after a race before but I am so glad I did. It was wonderful to share the cheers and joy with my fellow competitors from the other side of the barricades. I was proud and happy for every single one of them.

Marathon #24 – The Santa Clarita Marathon, 2012

A Big Hug To My 30s

The second time I ran the Santa Clarita Marathon was November 4, 2012. It was our 6th wedding anniversary, and the first time I had run a "stand alone" marathon in three years. I had not run a marathon with fresh legs in a while. I felt like a born-again virgin. It was more exciting than I anticipated because I put no expectations on myself; I just wanted to run as fast as I could.

When I was warming up at the starting line, I picked out a tight and toned, spiffy-looking blonde girl in neon pink shorts, who was a few feet in front of me, to be my rabbit. I knew if I could stay close to her, I would be in good shape. I started off the first few miles moving at a quick, but a sensible, 7:30ish minute per mile pace. Then my brain scrambled, "What? That is *not* sensible for me!" I rolled with it, because if I blew up, I blew up. I would crawl across the finish line if I had to. I had nothing to lose.

I clocked my fastest half-marathon that day, 1:37. My previous personal record was 1:40 at a stand-alone half-marathon, so I knew my day was going well. I did encounter a very uncomfortable burning sensation on the balls of my feet around mile fifteen, which was most likely a pitfall of wearing my swift minimalist lightweight shoes, an annoying side effect of running lighter and faster than usual. In any case, I slowed my pace a bit between miles seventeen and twenty because of the pain. Also, that is the lonely part of the course where we marathoners are out on the bike path with no half-marathoners to distract us, and barely any supporters to cheer for us. Suddenly, it clicked in my head that the faster I ran through this icky section, the sooner I would be back into the fold of the swift runners, so I sucked up the pain in my feet and dropped my pace back down to sub-eight minute miles.

When I saw that my watch was barely reading three hours at the twenty-three mile marker, I laughed out loud. It was insane. I had never run that fast in a marathon! I almost asked a volunteer if I was on the right part of the course, afraid that maybe I had cut it somehow. No, it was just that at thirty-three years old, I was finally a fast runner.

I finished the race in 3:28, nine minutes faster than my Boston Marathon qualifying time, 1st in my age group, and 4th overall female. "What?" "I know!!" I was on a high. I could not believe it—and it was my wedding anniversary to boot!! Sadly, Marion and I had to celebrate on Skype because he was still working in Montreal. Nevertheless, it was still a very special day; I was finally the runner I had always dreamed I would be. *Cheers to my mid-thirties!!*

Marathon #25 – Carlsbad, 2013

Best Phone Call EVER

As the tough and meaningful year of 2012 was ending and a fresh 2013 was around the corner, I decided to start it off with a bang by racing the Carlsbad Marathon again in late January. I decided to race Carlsbad because it hit three very important criteria: 1. Free accommodations. (I could stay with Mary and Jim.) 2. Within driving distance. ('Twas only two hours down the coast.), 3. I knew the course, and would hopefully run it faster this second time around.

When race weekend approached, it turned out to be fairly hectic for all of us because Hannah had two large events going on: testing for her high school placement exam, and a club volleyball tournament. The test took place in the morning at Hannah's dream school, Notre Dame Academy in Sherman Oaks, but we still had to hustle to get her to her tournament on time. Luckily, the tournament was in Anaheim, California which is between L.A. and Carlsbad, so I was able to catch at least one match or two before I needed to jet down to my final destination of the night.

The tournament schedule was running behind, which

meant I was only able to watch one match. They lost, but Hannah played great. However, even though her play was great, what was more apparent was that she was hitting her mid-teens in full force. She was in the thick of her friends for most of the pre-game prep time, and barely gave a wave to Marion and me as we watched longingly from the bleachers. I would like to say that I took her behavior in stride and was not hurt by getting the brush-off, but the fact is I was hurt. I knew this day would come, but I could have waited a little longer. Fortunately, I couldn't dwell on it for too long because I needed to drive down to Carlsbad in order to make the last few minutes of the expo in order to pick up my race bib and self-esteem.

The upside to my drive down south was that once again I would be bunking with my big sister, Mary, and her husband, Jim. On this particular Saturday night I was the lucky observer in their first attempt at cooking French onion soup. It was truly a labor of love. It took at least three hours to slice, simmer, and serve the tasty soup. I stuck with my usual pre-race pancake dinner, but the soup seemed magnificent in every measure imaginable.

One of the benefits of the marathon dinner prep was that it gave us ample time to spill our guts about everything going on in our lives, and simply enjoy being together. Once again, I'm sure my parents are re-reading that sentence in shock that I would ever feel so warm and fuzzy about Mary because of our battlefield-laden childhood, but my words and sentiments are true. Mary is a true friend, and the greatest sister in the universe. However, little did we know it was not just the three of us that night. A newly sprouted soul was waiting to surprise us all just a few weeks later; Mary was unknowingly pregnant with my niece, Darby.

I told Mary that she and Jim should enjoy their day off together, and not to worry about going out to cheer me on this time around. I was just happy to have spent another special night with my sister, and it turned out to be one for the history books. Less than two weeks later I received my favorite phone call of all time, "Taryn, I'm pregnant!"

I woke up on race morning to a drizzle in the air that I was not too psyched about, but I figured I had never run a marathon in the rain before, so I guessed this was my turn. I was excited about the race as always, but I was also curious to know if the newfound speed I discovered at the Santa Clarita Marathon was just a fluke, or whether it would pop up again. The race organizers handed out plastic trash bags for us to protect ourselves from the precipitation that always seems to surprise SoCal residents. Rain?? I peeled off my trash bag while walking to the start because even though it was a comfy insulator from the rain, I wanted to run as fast as I could, for as long as I could, and a trash bag flapping in the wind would only slow me down.

I always appreciate running a course for the second or third time. I believe that kind familiarity is priceless. It lends confidence to push hard and have faith that my body will know what to do and where to go. The race started early again, 6 a.m. I felt great, and cruised along the first 10K of the race passing most of my competitors until I found my groove with the 3:15 pace group. Yep, that happened. The weather was perfect. The rain stopped, which left the air cool but not cold. My plan was to keep my pace around 7:00 minute miles for as long as I could hang on, then I would try to keep it below 8:00 minute miles for the rest of the race and finish in as close to one piece as possible.

I met a few nice fellows around mile seven or so who were on running quests of their own. It was fun to share my 35 by 35 story, and be cheered on and respected by my peers. Then my competitive nature kicked in and I dropped them. I cranked through the first half-marathon in 1:36, beating my personal best for a stand-alone half-marathon, so I knew that day would be something special. Maybe my Santa Clarita speediness was not a fluke?

I ran through some uncomfortable miles between fifteen and eighteen, again my toughest spot on this course. They have us run out on a coarsely paved highway for a four-mile out-and-back that tends to play mind games more than anything else, but I just took each step with measured pace and kept my eyes up and ahead.

Soon enough I was screaming down the hill just after mile eighteen and meeting up with all of the half-marathoners who careen in to the course at that point of the race. I did not like that crushing, crowded sensation the first time I ran this race, and I did not like it now. However, I felt too good to be upset about anything. I looked down at my watch around mile twenty-one and tried to do the math in my head of what my finish time would be if I fell to a 10-minute pace for the last few miles, 3:25... "Wow!!" I was stunned, because even though I am terrible at math, I thought I had that figure right, which meant if I maintained my current pace I could go under 3:25... "*WHAT!!??*" I smiled like I was in my own little world among thousands, and then picked up the pace to try to finish under 3:25.

The last mile or so was a series of twists and turns, then a marvelous downhill that led us through a path of cheering fans on toward the finish line. I stormed down the hill like the large-legged lady I am, and leaped across the line with a huge grin. I looked down at my watch... 3:23!! I was beside myself with glee, I couldn't believe it, but there it was in its honest-to-goodness, Garmin-gleamed-glory: I had cracked 3:25 hours. *Wow.*

I had never enjoyed a drive on the 5 freeway more than I did that day on my way home. I sat in traffic with a smile plastered across my face, reveling in my fast time, and plotting to go even faster next time. Then it hit me. I had just finished my twenty-fifth marathon. Only ten more to go...

Taryn Spates

Marathon #26 – The Orange County Marathon, 2013

Getting Faster

The winter of 2013 was packed. There were lots of volleyball tournaments with Hannah, we had a new Weimaraner puppy, Blueberry Wheat (we name all of our dogs after beer), and most importantly, Marion was home from Montreal! (*I invite all of you to stop reading for a moment and go hug your favorite loved one. It's okay, I know you'll pick up where you left off. It feels good, right?*) I didn't want to let Marion out of my sight for the first few weeks he was home. It was just so nice to look to my right while watching TV and see him sitting there. I loved him a lot before he left, but to be apart from your partner for that long really puts priorities in perspective, and I vowed to never take our marriage for granted. Every moment together since has been a gift. I am not perfect, and neither is he, but we are perfect for each other.

As soon as spring had sprung, another marathon was upon me. I ran my twenty-sixth marathon on Cinco de Mayo 2013 in lovely Orange County, California. I was on another solo mission because we had Marion's family arriving that night, and he needed to receive and entertain them, so just after 2 p.m. I packed up my pancakes and drove south toward the cool ocean air of Newport Beach.

I arrived at the host hotel around 4 p.m., but by 7 p.m. I was wrestling with a blistering case of hotel fever and decided to venture on a walkabout around the hotel. This sort of "mini-adventure" had become one of my favorite activities after my dad took me on a business trip to Washington, D.C. when I was ten. We stayed at the JW Marriott, where he would let me explore the hotel and its adjoining mall for hours by myself while he was in business meetings. Keep in mind this was 1990, and I was a tall girl even then, so I don't think I was an easy target. But to answer your question: would I let Hannah go exploring on her own even now at sixteen? Uh, no. That said, I am thankful my dad gave me that freedom because I think that trip gave me a shot of independence that shaped my confidence for the rest of my life. Hence, my many inspired solo missions to endurance events around the world.

Once I ventured outside my room, I found an adorable couple taking photos at the gazebo just beyond the pool, and offered to take one of the two of them. We chatted for a while and it turned out they were running the race the next day as well, and it was the wife's first marathon. Yum, a newbie! I jumped right into telling her all of the amazing sensations she would feel during the race, the pain: the glory, the fatigue, the tears. She looked a tad bewildered, but I think she appreciated my enthusiasm. Her husband asked me what my goal time was, and before I could think I blurted out, "3:20."

"Wow, that's awesome—good luck!"

"Thanks, you too." I smiled and turned back toward the lobby and said out loud to myself, "What did I just say?" Then a cool confidence washed over me and I said it again, internally this time, "3:20."

The start time was a ludicrous 5:30 a.m., hence the hotel stay, but I was pleasantly surprised to discover that the starting line was literally in front of my hotel. Sweet! The mood was stirring because this race was only two weeks after the Boston Marathon bombings. Security was tight, and the race director held a moment of silence for the victims just before the gun went off. While standing in silence, I felt my chest heat up, and tears swell, because runners are a family, and we were hurting as a family, but we would rise above and beyond the terror together for the next 26.2 miles.

I took off quickly and kept my pace at 6:45 minute miles for the first two or three, and thought to myself, maybe early starts aren't so bad after all. I felt strong and consistent for the first eight miles. I looked at my watch and saw it said 1:00. Excellent. I even passed a super speedy tiny blond girl who had beaten me a few months earlier in Santa Clarita (the one in the pink shorts, remember her?). My confidence was high, but I wanted to remain calm and just do the work in order to finish strong, and faster than ever before.

I accepted the challenge in those early miles that this was a race of strategy, and it was time to lay down a dominating routine for my marathons. Around mile ten or so I hopped on the heels of a slight-framed Asian man in his early 50s, I would guess, who was carving through the course by choosing the perfect angles to reduce wasting time and energy. I was thrilled to be in the front row of this real world class on tactics.

I maintained a sub 7:40 minute mile pace for the back-end ten miles of the race, where it really gets tough, just after mile sixteen. My body felt strong, but my feet were burning up, a small price to pay for choosing minimalist racing shoes. I knew this would be a fast race for me, but I felt more like a rule-abiding intern than a risk-taker. I did not want to be overzealous, but I should have switched on my animal instinct to make real headway. Instead, I bided my time. I worked my way up the field and watched fellow females peel away as I passed them, which was great, but I questioned myself. "Could I have done more?"

I passed the 3:15 pacer just around mile twenty-five. Don't get too excited; his group had already dropped him. I knew I was close to something special—3:20 was now in my sights— but mile twenty-five went on for an eternity. Even though I cranked up my pace to catch up with my expectations, I knew I was just outside of my goal, and would be finishing over 3:20. When I rounded that dreadful twenty-six mile corner and still had .2 miles to go, my legs opened up, but my heart sank. The clock said it all. 3:23 hours. I walked through the finish chute and found a large tree to lean my legs on, when some gentleman walked up to me and said,

"You were the 6th overall female!"

"Wow, thanks."

I was 35% pleased with my performance and 65% disappointed. I didn't push hard enough. I could have, I *should* have done more. Why didn't I? Then I remembered that I was in the middle of this *monumental* quest, and this race was only twenty-six of thirty-five. I still had a ways to go. I needed to be smart. I was asking a lot of my body, and should not be greedy. I would have another crack at going for 3:20 again soon enough. Only two measly Ironmans stood in the way of another stand-alone marathon starting line.

Taryn Spates

Marathon #27 – Vineman, 2013

Great Day at the Races

As I have progressed over the years as an athlete and fortunate able-bodied human being, I have tried to up the ante with my goals every chance I get, and the summer of 2013 was a doozy. I signed up to race Ironman Wisconsin the previous year because, as I have discussed ad nauseum, one needs to sign up early for such races. However, Vineman, my favorite grassroots long distance triathlon, does not require the same sense of urgency. I registered in early March that year for Vineman because I thought racing in two Ironman triathlons within six weeks of each other would be a meaningful challenge. It was.

As we are all well aware by now, Vineman is an iron-distance triathlon which takes place in the amazing northern California wine country. Even though I was very excited to race, I did not place too much pressure on myself because my "A" race was still a few weeks away in Madison, Wisconsin. Therefore, Vineman was just meant to test-drive the machine, work out some kinks, and enjoy the day.

I rented an adorable house in Monte Rio, a tiny town west

of Guerneville. All I can say is, I love Monte Rio, and you should all go there as soon as possible. It is heavenly. The days leading up to the race were wonderful because I spent some quality time with Peter's and Tim's families (all of their children are delectable), and cherished some alone time that included an epic drive to the coast. It was one of those drives that had me pondering life and my purpose in it, as only gorgeous drives through the forest to the sea can. Then just as I was starting to get a tad antsy, my Prince Charming arrived. Marion flew in Friday morning the day before the race.

However, on Friday afternoon just as I walked through the front door after spending the afternoon at the race expo, I noticed my back tire was flat. Since I have tubular tires, I could not make a simple tube change. I had to drive back to the expo and rent an alternate wheel. This mini-adventure was both annoying and liberating because I felt like I had already survived my spell of trouble even before the gun went off. Therefore, I could relax and spend the rest of my Friday night/Race Eve prepping my mind, body and soul for the crushing day ahead.

The dawn of race morning was calm and cloudy, the same conditions I had experienced at my first two Vineman races. I felt right in my wheelhouse, chatting up competitors while setting my bike up in the transition area. Every nuance felt familiar. I was fit, and anxious to see what I could do.

The river was very low that year, but I was moving along just fine. I was not surprised in the slightest when I saw the clock read 1:14, my usual swim time for this course. I quickly ran to my bike in the transition area, tussled with my Rocket

Science wetsuit, and noticed there were many, many bikes still on the rack. "Yes!" I was ecstatic, because that meant there were many more women still roaming in the river. As I climbed onto my bike and pedaled the mini-hill out of transition, I saw Marion off to the left behind the barriers and yelled, "How many silver caps?!"

"Not many! *Go!*" he shouted with a respectful balance of reassurance and authority, and off I rode with a smile.

The silver caps is a reference to all of the ladies in my swim group, ages 30 – 44. Or maybe more than that — in basic terms, my competition. The bike course is a two-loop, fifty-six mile ride through the breathtaking vineyards and farms that outline Sonoma County. I pushed my pace hard from the start, having faith in my fitness, and not at all considering the marathon I had to run after I was finished with this fabulous spin through wine country. I have found this is a great mental tactic in order to stay present, because if I think about how huge the day is, my head might explode.

The first miracle of the day occurred when I was up and over the *big* climb up Chalk Hill Road. On my way to finishing my first loop heading back to town, I heard, "Go Taryn!!" It was my stepbrother Chris, his wife, Debbie, and their daughter Sidney! I could not believe they had found such a perfect spot on the bike course, especially since this was their first triathlon spectating experience; I was very impressed. It is amazing the impact that hearing your own name gives you when you're deep into a race. It is like a shot of adrenaline and love, the perfect confidence booster.

The "Spectacular Spectator" awards continued when I

was starting out again on my second loop and heard screaming voices streaming out of a car careening straight toward me. It was Peter, Alexa and their amazing kiddos, Kaia and Reed. They cheered, and sped away from me to find a place to pull over farther down the road. When I caught up to them pedaling up a short hill, Peter yelled, "This is your day!" A wave of happiness hit me because I felt so thankful to be right where I was, right when I was, enjoying the fruits of years of dreaming and training to actually live my dream.

When I rolled into the transition area ready to start the marathon, I had a sense I was in a good spot. There were almost no bikes on my rack, but I did not have a watch on the bike either, so the first time I saw the time it was when I put on my GPS watch to start the run. It read 1:43 p.m., which was wonderful. I knew that if I could run my marathon like I was capable of running it, I would finish the race in under eleven hours, which had been my goal for the last three years.

I started the run feeling good. I saw my whole family on the first of three loops as we exited Windsor High School, Peter taking his cue to run alongside me as always and assess how I was feeling. I was feeling good, but I needed to make a pit stop just to ensure a comfortable run, always a wise if not needful choice.

I was cranking away sub-eight miles for the first three miles or so, sifting my way through the large crowd of mainly female half-ironman racers, participating in the all-female event, Barb's Race. Suddenly, I was alone. I had seen the first-place woman screaming down the opposite side of the road about ten minutes prior, then about five to ten minutes later I saw another woman, but that was it. I did not need confirmation that I was in third place, but I wanted it. I yelled out to one of the volunteers near our turnaround point to ask how many girls she had seen. "You're number three!" I couldn't believe I heard those words out loud; I was in third place!

Fortunately, this was not my first rodeo on this course; I knew there was still a lot of the race left to run. Once I started to pass by mile eight, all was not looking well. I took a couple of salt tabs even though we completely lucked out with amazing eighty-degree temperatures, plus I was drinking water and sports drink. But my tum-tum was getting a little grumbly.

Let me go back a bit to explain. I had prepped my bike to eat two energy bars, two packages of chews, and a gel during the bike leg. Well, I lost one of the energy bars early during the ride, and after feeling dizzy and nearly falling asleep in the aero position, I opted to eat a couple of the energy bars they were passing out at the aid stations—not my usual brand—a brutal necessity at the time and one that came back to haunt me on the run. My GI system did not react well to the menu change. Thankfully, I was finishing up my first loop and would be replenished by positivity from my family along the sidewalks as I ran in to start my second loop.

I did regain my composure after a few high-fives from Peter and Marion, but once I was back in the incessant hills of Windsor, I needed to stop again and take a twenty-second time out. When I emerged from the port-o-let, I felt a sense of strength and renewal, but I was sure that I had lost my third place position. Oh well, my new focus was to just finish my twenty-seventh marathon.

When I finished my second loop, around mile seventeen, my immediate future was not looking so great. At this point I had one singular goal: run to the next port-o-let. For the first time ever, I had to wait in line. Wonderful. It did not matter. I did my thing, took in some fuel at the two next aid stations, and finally around mile twenty a calm came over my stomach and I was ready to run my own race. I feel a little guilty saying this, but I was relieved to see that the closest girls behind me were looking a little rough too, so I believed with my renewed vigor I should be able to keep my third place finish.

For the last six miles I was in my zone. The tail-end of marathons are my favorite part of any race, especially in an Ironman. I looked at my watch and knew that I would be over eleven hours, but not by much, so I would push as hard as possible to finish strong. As I rounded the twenty-six mile marker, the crowd on the corner was quiet until I yelled, "This is it for me!" They erupted in cheers, and stood to clap for me loud and proud as I ran down the road to make another turn, then down to the finish line. Since the race was all about loops, there was a turn for the "2nd loop" and one for the "Finish." When I turned toward the finish option, the crowd around me started screaming. I heard Marion and Chris from the sideline, and sprinted in for my first podium finish at a triathlon.

I finished 3rd place overall female, and 1st in my 30-34 age group, with a time of 11:08 hours (four minutes faster than my previous best Ironman time) and a 3:59 marathon. That finally dipped me underneath the four-hour Ironman marathon boulder that had weighed on me for so long. Most importantly, I finished my twenty-seventh marathon. Only eight more to go until magical number thirty-five.

One of Alexa's great car photos around mile 60 of the bike leg

Marathon #28 – Ironman Wisconsin, 2013

Racing With My Hero

The precious six weeks that I spent in between Vineman and Ironman Wisconsin were filled with needful recovery, and a few hard and long workouts to keep me primed for another stellar effort. However, I placed a huge amount of pressure on myself going into Wisconsin, because this was my "A" race of the season, and the initial Ironman course I had been pining over for years. I wanted to improve on my time from Vineman and to try again to go under eleven hours, but more importantly I wanted to enjoy the entire experience, because my gut told me this would be the last Ironman I would compete in for a long time.

Following is a special treat. It is a look inside my mind just one day before the race, from an email I sent out to family and friends to thank them for their support:

Greetings Everyone,
I wanted to check in with all of you and give you a quick rundown of what I have been up to the past couple of days, and how

this Ironman is shaping up to be pretty special. First off, just after I landed on Thursday afternoon I was lucky enough to be taken on a tour of the bike course by the 2008 female Champion, Hillary Biscay, which was wonderful because not only does she know every inch of this course, this will be her seventh time racing this year. There is no way I could have found my way around that Wisconsin farmland on my own; the course is beautiful, but tough. Also, Hillary has been my coach and mentor throughout my Ironman journey, so it meant the world to me that she would carve out this time to show me around and prep me for this marvelous course!

The adventure continued as I got COMPLETELY lost on my way to my hotel. I was even pulled over by a cop for not having my lights on, but I found my way, and now I feel like I know Madison like the back of my hand. On Friday morning I set off for a mellow 40 min. run on a beautiful bike path near my hotel. As I was admiring the scenery, my left foot slipped off the uneven pavement and I went down hard on my left knee and right hand. Awesome! Also, I rolled my ankle. Oops. I walked on it for a minute, and decided to turn around and run back to my hotel. Fortunately, I did not feel any broken bones or see any black and blue, but my foot was more than tender and started to swell, so I was getting a little nervous. Next, I went to get coffee with a wonderful woman named Meghan Walsh, who is the contact for the charity I race for, AHOPE. She is fantastic, and we had a great morning, but my sore foot was in the back of my mind the whole visit.

Next up was going to the athlete meeting, and doing a little souvenir shopping back at Monona Terrace, the base camp for the race. I could move my foot around but it hurt, and I had to think for a minute about the busy rest of the year I have lined up. One more triathlon, and two more marathons. Did I want to risk all of that to

162

finish this race?

While I was shopping for Ironman goodies, I ran into a fellow member of my Big Sexy Racing triathlon team. Jedd is a fast fellow from a neighboring Wisconsin town who is gunning for a Kona slot in the 30-34 age group. I had only seen and spoken with him on Facebook, so it was great to catch up in person, and the bonus of all bonuses was that he is a Physical Therapist, and offered to examine my foot. Um...yes please! He gave me the "okay" to race, because even though I did have swelling, my mobility was good, and there was nothing broken. Sweet!

I spent the rest of the evening eating my pre-race feast of healthy delectables from a local co-op, and icing and moving my foot around. By the time I went to bed, I felt about 200% better than I did in the morning. Even though my hand and knee were still bloodied like an eight-year-old tomboy, my foot felt ready to go.

So, here we are on "day before the race" morning, and I have one small bike ride to do in order to warm up my legs and make sure my bike is ready to rock. Then, it is just dropping off all of my gear, a pancake feast tonight, and hopefully a few hours of sleep before I am up at 4 a.m. and ready for another amazing day outside.

If you have a minute or two on Sunday, you can track me on www.ironman.com, there will be a link for IM Wisconsin, then go to Live Tracking, and plug in my bib# 516 to find me. Also, Hillary's # is 41, and Maik is #1... My $ is on him for the win, and for Hillary to be close to the front, too. I am going to push hard all day, but for this ninth IM of mine I am just happy to be lining up and enjoying the day.

If you made it through this whole email, thank you! Also, thank you for the amazing support and inspiration you all have given me throughout these many years of endurance events, I really appreciate it.

> *Love,*
> *Iron T*

The race started with a valiant effort in Lake Monona for the swim. I was excited and angry because it was the most violent swim I had ever experienced in an Ironman. And the punches to my head, and back were consistent the entire 2.4 miles. When I glanced at the clock after finally reaching the shore I smiled, 1:14, of course. Next, I ran up the many spiraling levels of the Monona Terrace parking structure, then inside the center itself to change into my bike gear, and off I went toward the hills and farmland of Wisconsin.

I loved every pedal stroke of the course. There were a bounty of rolling hills that catered to my strengths, and endless grasslands in every direction. It was a beautiful bike ride. I played sling-shot with a fellow female racer for about twenty miles, but at the halfway mark, she was safely in my rearview. There were stretches of rough roads that rattled my bike and nerves for miles, but I maintained my pace, determined to give Madison more than everything I had. This race had been on my mind for six years, and now the day had finally arrived — I wanted to enjoy every minute of it.

The second loop of the bike course felt faster than the first. I was in a "take no prisoners" rhythm, which meant I had pity for no one on the course, least of all myself. There was one male racer who must have had a traumatic experience with a strong woman in his life, because he could not get with the program that once you get passed, you have to drop back and allow that stronger rider their earned position. This guy just kept leap-frogging me whenever I overcame him, and finally I just let him go and live with the misery of over-worked legs for the marathon. I was happy settling into a spin out session over the last few miles in order to set up a smart, strong marathon.

The crowds along this run route are mighty from mile one. A definite highlight was being able to run around the football field at University of Wisconsin, twice. The two-loop course suited me well, because I always push myself further once I am familiar with a course. I did not see Maik along the course at all—he was way too far ahead—but I did see Hillary at around mile seven, and it felt wonderful to be able to cheer for her this time around.

Every mile hurt, but the kind of hurt I crave. I was not running fast, but clicking off consistent sub-nine minute miles, and passing people left and right. Luckily, my ankle felt fine, or maybe I just refused to acknowledge the pain; either way it did not bother me at all. The last few miles of the race were overwhelming. I had no idea where I ranked, but my time was excellent, especially considering I had raced a Vineman only six weeks prior. I did not want it to end, but it did. I crossed the finish in a haze of disbelief. I finished in 11:13; it wasn't my best time, but it was definitely my best day. I slurped every second of that race and felt like I could have done more. I could have kept going, I wanted to, but it was done. The only option was to revel in another Ironman finish, then get my act together, and go home.

I am thrilled to report that Maik did indeed take the win, and Hillary raced valiantly as always, while I placed 5th in my age group, my best place to date in an Ironman. I fought hard in the swim, rode hard on the bike, and ran as fast as I could though the campus of University of Wisconsin. I wavered at times, but the crowds were everywhere on the course, keeping my heart beating and legs moving when my mind wanted them to stop. I am proud to have finally raced in Ironman Wisconsin, six years after trying to get there for my first Ironman. I probably won't ever race there again, but never say never.

Marathon # 29 – The Santa Clarita Marathon, 2013

Third Time Is The Charm

Just two months after Ironman Wisconsin, and only two weeks after a haphazard Olympic distance triathlon race in San Diego, I decided to run my 29th marathon in Santa Clarita; hoping the third time would be the charm. It was a beautiful day, I gained an hour of sleep because of the switch to Standard Time, which was helpful, but I honestly had no idea how I would feel when I trotted down to the starting line in my blaring neon compression socks and neon running shoes. I was excited to run fast, but for how long could I keep it up? That would be the grand mystery of the day.

The gun went off after a glorious rendition of the national anthem sung by a 7th grader, an amazing talent indeed. I started off quickly; my goal was to maintain a 7:30 minute mile average throughout the day. That would have me finishing at around 3:15, a solid six-minute personal best for me, and a big ask. But I figured, why not just run hard and let the chips fall where they may?

I was cruising comfortably at a 7:10ish pace for the first

eleven miles, then around mile thirteen I unknowingly slowed my pace a bit. "Hmm, this feels different." I was in third place, but then a quick young runner passed me. I could tell because she was wearing a cotton t-shirt and her calves were yet to be chiseled in the marvelous way long hours on the road tend to do, but I was honestly impressed by her effort, and cheered her on as she passed me by.

I looked at my watch more than I should have between miles fifteen and nineteen, but I could not resist because I felt like I was moving quickly. But my watch did not lie; I was not. I knew my chips were cashed in between mile twenty-one and twenty-two at a turnaround spot where I watched three girls running up seconds behind me looking strong, and no doubt in much better spirits than I was. I kid you not, one of the runners was wearing *full* makeup. But I cheered them on as they passed me one by one, they deserved it. At this point in the race I was feeling the mental and physical fatigue of running six marathons in one year, two of which were within Ironmans. Knowing I had one more left in just five weeks, a trail marathon no less (*gulp*), I just gathered myself and decided to finish feeling solid, and not ripped to shreds.

Unfortunately, I came upon a fretful sight just after the mile twenty-four marker. It was the cotton T-shirt girl. "Uh-oh, she should be way farther ahead than where she is right now." When I came upon her, she had stopped running altogether and had that creamy-colored crust of dehydration slathered all over her face. She was surrounded by two friends on their bikes, but they only had water, and she needed electrolytes stat! I stopped to offer all the nutrition I had on me, but she said she said her stomach hurt, and waved me on, so I ran off with a quickened pace, praying that there would be some medics at the mile twenty-five aid station. Yep, there they were, "Hey, there is a girl about a half mile back who needs electrolytes!" I think they heard me, because I saw them pedal off in her direction, but I was still on the clock, so I kept running toward the finish line.

At less than a mile out, I started to feel good. I knew my PR wishes were blown, but I would still finish with a decent time, especially considering the year I had put into my legs. I opted to take it all in while smiling, cheering fellow runners on, and enjoying myself as I rounded the final few turns toward the finish line.

I finished in 3:30, just two minutes slower than my previous race there a year before, which had been my turning point marathon. Still, I was pretty happy with twenty-nine. Not my best day, but I pushed hard early, hung on to the end, and moved one race closer to my goal.

Taryn Spates

Marathon #30 – North Face Trail Marathon

A New Challenge

I ran my 30th marathon on December 7, 2013. I ran the 26.2 miles through the rightfully famed and epically gorgeous Marin Headlands in San Francisco, California. The race is called the North Face Challenge because it is sponsored by North Face, and there are many different distances offered to "challenge" oneself. I chose my old standby marathon distance, but there were 50K and 50-mile races offered that day as well. I felt a little wussy choosing half the distance of the longest one offered, 26.2 miles, but I just can't quit my sweet 26.2.

I registered for this race in early February 2013. I was intrigued because it was going to be a real challenge for me. I knew the course was tough from talking with friends who had run it before, and I felt for the first time in a while a twinge of butterflies in my stomach when I clicked "Register" on the website. I was nervous and actually fearful, but still excited to learn more about running and myself through training and competing in this race.

The specific trail training I ran before this race could be described as minimal at best. I had run the Santa Clarita Marathon on November 3, so I had only five weeks to properly prep for this race with putting in long runs in the hills. I did crank out some great runs, but I should have done much, much more in the months prior to race day. I had a ball discovering new trails above the YMCA where I swim, and galloping across familiar trails from my years on the Claremont Cross Country team (Go Wolfpack!). However, this running life is its own journey, so now I know that running on trails is valuable throughout the year, not just five weeks before a trail marathon.

The early December morning of race day was cold but sunny. I met many amazing people as we hovered together around a heat lamp before heading off to the start line where Ultra-Marathon Man himself, Dean Karnazes, led us in a quick pep talk and then waved us all good luck before we ran into nature.

The course can be described in three words: hilly, beautiful, and...hilly. I was not surprised by the hills, but they were steep and went up for miles. I chose my strategy quickly: *keep running for as long as humanly possible*. That may seem obvious, but most of my cohorts succumbed to walking up the hills during the first couple of miles, and I was not going to go along with the crowd this time around. I had learned my lesson after Catalina to not follow the herd, but rather to trust my instincts. I knew I had enough strength to run most of the way — not necessarily speed as this was not a personal record course — but I kept chipping away every mile at my own perceived effort and picking off "walkers" from mile five on.

There was a section of the race between miles fifteen through nineteen where we descended down to and subsequently climbed up from Muir Beach, and shared the course with the 50-milers and 50K runners. They were all studs, and I was humbled to briefly be running among them, but what I noticed was that most, if not all, of them were walking, and just looked dreadful. On the other hand, I felt good. Well, let me rephrase that. My masochistic twin, "Terry," was in full effect from mile seventeen on, and I started to enjoy the grind. I may have felt good, but I probably looked terrible too.

The finish line snuck up on me because one of the girls I met before the race said the race was slightly over 26.2 miles. So I was tracking my Garmin meticulously, and was shocked when the finish line coincided with just over twenty-five miles on my watch. Nevertheless, I burst down the last mini-hill through the finish chute with a broad smile, and cheerful quads. The relentless beating they had withstood for the last 4:41 hours was finally over!

Moreover, the real bonus to this endurance-infused weekend in San Francisco was visiting with my sister Sarah, and cheering her on for her first marathon in Sacramento at the California International Marathon the following Sunday. Sarah has always been very special to me and it was a real honor to play a role in helping her train for, and ultimately crush, the race. Plus, I was able to meet her super-cyclist boyfriend, Eric, and geek out in bike talk for a minute with him, something I rarely get to do. Then I got to spend some quality time with my stepbrother, Chris, as we were "spectators in arms" along the charming streets of Sacramento, rooting Speedy Sarah on to her *first* marathon finish.

Overall, the weekend was a challenge in time management, and luckily I was able to squeeze in a couple of hours visiting with Peter, Alexa, and my amazing niece and nephew, Kaia and Reed, on my way back from Sacramento. The running force is strong in them, too.

Marathon #31 – The Honkers Marathon

Finding The Formula

It is a fascinating fact that, after running thirty marathons, I finally figured it out how to do it right on my thirty-first. I ran the Honkers Marathon in Anaheim, California, (yep, Mickey and Minnie's hometown) on January 12, 2014. I chose Honkers because it was small and new, and because the previous year's winner had run a 3:33, so I thought I might even walk away with a bit of the prize purse. Furthermore, I was excited to run a marathon on the road again. No more dirt for me, please.

I left our house at 4:30 a.m. in order to make the 6:00 a.m. registration and 7:00 a.m. start time. The freeways were clear at such an early hour, a fleeting and cherished feeling when driving in southern California. I met the race director a few minutes before the start. She was standing with her two "twenty-something" children. They beamed standing next to her; they were so proud. It was very special to witness, and of course I was honored to meet her, too. She was excited that I had chosen Honkers to be one of my thirty-five marathons, and wished me luck as we all made our way up to the starting line.

I was hyped up for too many reasons to mention, but on the top of my list was that this would be my first marathon wearing my Smash Fast n' Loud triathlon top. It was hot off my old coach (and constant hero) Hillary Biscay's fashion line. I knew I looked amazing, and hoped that added confidence would give me an edge over my not-so-dazzlingly-dressed competition. I am sure those girls were fast, but I won "best dressed" hands down.

The marathoners were mixed in with the half-marathoners so I was not sure who my exact competition really was, but I blasted off of the line quicker than usual, which felt wonderful. My last race had been the trail marathon in San Francisco, which was epic but not fast at all, so it was a real treat to be able to open my stride up and rip it from the start.

I held my pace steady at 7:15 minute mile pace until mile ten, and then I started to slow down a bit. The upside was that my energy was high and I had finally figured out a solid fueling plan. After thirty marathons, I had cracked the code! Unfortunately, I could only hang onto that pace for so long. Not even a million energy chews could keep the needle hanging over the red line much longer. At this point I believe I was in second place. I was a little annoyed when a super-gangly, white-as-porcelain lady running like Rachel in that classic *Friends* episode zoomed past me. She was wearing shoes the size and shape of cinder blocks, her arms and legs flailing all around her like a helicopter. Oh well, I thought, you go, girl!

The course wound its way up the bike path for miles. I would like to say there were plenty of water stops, but there were few, and *very* far between. I zoned out a bit, listening to the buzzing traffic coming from the 5 freeway just off the course, but I snapped back into reality around mile eighteen when it hit me: I am going to finish in the top three today. I was smiling when I passed volunteers, and clapped in awe and sincere respect when the leader passed me at the mile twenty-one turn-around. Girlfriend was petite, toned, and at least a decade older than me, and she was movin'!

I passed a couple guys on the last stretch of the bike path mainly because I had more experience than they did. Chances are homeboy in the green soccer shorts had not run half a dozen marathons in the last six months, but guess who had? That is what this race was for me: recognition that all of the lessons I had learned from my first thirty marathons were paying off in my thirty-first. I ate one energy chew every four miles starting at mile five, and then ate a gel at mile twenty-one, and felt strong the whole day. I chased down whoever I could chase down because I was patient and knew even from a distance that my pace was faster. I would catch up and pass them before the finish line.

I felt cool and calculated the whole morning, but leaped out of my sleek façade when I rounded the last corner and finished in 3:23, a very respectable time considering the wear and tear on my legs at that point in my schedule. I placed 3rd overall female, and was congratulated by the race director quickly after I crossed the line. She asked me for feedback about the course, so I told her that more water stations were needed along the bike path. She responded defensively, "Oh really, you know some parts of the course are hard to get volunteers all the way out there for, but I will take that into consideration, thank you." There was no need to sugarcoat it: if I thought it was dry out there, I am sure most of the other runners did too.

I am not sure if I will ever run the Honkers Marathon again, but I am very glad I did. It is always nice to support smaller, grassroots-type races, like Vineman and the Cowtown Marathon. I enjoy the massive, glitzy ones too, but the smaller ones are closest to my heart.

Marathon #32 – The Los Angeles Marathon, 2014

I Love LA

There is something about walking among thousands of like-minded people before dawn at one of the most iconic locations in the country that gets me really excited and makes me happy. This was how I felt on the morning of March 9, 2014 at Dodger Stadium, milling around the starting line of my thirty-second marathon, the Los Angeles Marathon. This would be the second time I raced L.A. The first time was only my second marathon ever back in 2003, and I had never really wanted to run it again because the course was not very pleasant. However, about four or five years ago they changed the course to be a point-to-point, starting at Dodger Stadium high above downtown, and finishing right above the beach in Santa Monica, running through Hollywood, West Hollywood, Beverly Hills and Westwood all the way to the finish. It was a true tour of L.A., a work of staggering genius. I had spent years driving over every single inch of it, and now it was time for me to run over all of it.

I lucked out because I was seeded in the B corral, which

was near the starting line just behind the super-fast elite runners. This meant I did not have to battle thousands of runners to find my place and pace early, like I had during my first go-around in '03. This time I was running quickly and freely right from the gun, *yee-haw!* You may never meet another human being more in love with her hometown than I am with Los Angles. I love the people. We are not all snobs and jerks. The traffic is constant, but the side streets are plentiful, and a little creativity and patience pay off huge when driving around town. I have lived in Venice, West Hollywood, Playa Del Rey, North Hollywood, and now Granada Hills, plus I grew up in outlying Claremont to the east, and Palos Verdes to the south, so I know my way around my beloved city, and I am the first to show outsiders how amazing she really is. Just ask for a tour — I will make the time. In fact, one of the silliest jobs I ever had was as a driver for a visiting music executive from New York. She didn't want to deal with driving herself around L.A. traffic, but couldn't afford a limo driver, so this redhead in a Civic fit the bill just fine. Obviously, this was BU — Before Uber.

I was especially excited for this race. Since it was as local as a race would ever be, Marion would be able to cheer me on at the halfway point, just past mile thirteen on the Sunset Strip, and he would be there at the finish line to drive me home, *yay*. I hope we will be able to run this race together one of these years; I think he has it in him for sure.

The sky was absolutely stunning just before the start; we were in for a glorious day. The first five or so miles flew by in a flash. We thundered downhill from Dodgers Stadium through Chinatown, and around downtown and up a sheer steep hill right next to the Disney Performing Arts Center. I was slightly prepared for it, but that hill was tough for all of us. Then we trucked over a couple of freeway overpasses and ran up and down some rolling hills into Los Feliz and Silverlake, where hipsters spilled out from the cafes, drinking their espressos and looking befuddled at the great stampede swarming their beloved Los Feliz Boulevard. I can honestly say that I was happier to be running a marathon than sitting outside on a patio.

I felt wonderful. I was not cooking my legs too much, and it was around mile ten or so, over the first stretch along Hollywood Boulevard. Oh, how I love this street! I have been in love with movies and movie-making since I was ten years old, and I have had a laser focus on becoming a producer ever since, so I have always felt butterflies in my belly when I am on Hollywood Boulevard. However, this Sunday was even cooler than most, because the Oscars were just a week before, and we ran right by the Dolby Theatre where Jordan Catalano's tresses were just a week out of my reach. Unfortunately, right around mile twelve, as we ran down to Sunset, I started to feel a little off. Nothing crazy, just slower, and slightly off my pace. Then, I saw Marion jumping around in his Chargers jersey just past Crescent Heights on the north side of Sunset, and my heart and legs sprang back to life. He was taking photos, yelling and screaming my name. It was wonderful, and exactly what I needed to get me through that dreaded "valley" on the course.

The next four or five miles took us down through Rodeo

Drive in Beverly Hills (I felt so fancy), then on out toward the Westside along Wilshire Boulevard. This was a neat part of the course because for at least 100 to 200 yards, we were surrounded on both sides by cheerleading squads from local high schools. I was feeling pretty good, but the day was heating up fast, so my "pretty good" turned into "not-so good" pretty quickly.

The aid/water stations were plentiful and consistent along the course, except when we entered the VA Medical Center property around mile twenty in Westwood. This was a long, exposed stretch of the course with an annoying hill thrown in for good measure to really test our grit, which I respected but was not too fond of. I was gaining popularity because I always carry salt tabs with me, and I gave a few of them to a once-speedy guy who stopped dead in his tracks right in front of me just before that nasty hill. He said "Thank you," but his searing eyes said so much more. Once we exited the VA, literally just feet off of their property was a water station staffed with energetic volunteers anxious to cool us off and cheer us on to the finish. Hallelujah!

The last four to five miles of the course was along the famously filmed San Vicente Boulevard. It was a little up and down most of the way, but I was able to open my stride with a mile to go and just rejoice that this race was almost over. As I turned the final corner onto Ocean Avenue, I sprinted in as fast as I could, taking full advantage of the heavy crowds, thick on both sides, cheering me on toward the finish line. I was thrilled with my results, because I ran much faster than I expected to, 3:25, and really had a blast the whole day. Once again, it was another great bonding experience with my lovely Los Angeles.

Taryn Spates

Marathon #33 – Griffith Park Trail Marathon, 2014

Running Above L.A.

I know it may seem that I live an adventurous, jet-setting life of a running enthusiast without a care in the world, but that is not the case at all. What I do have is a very supportive husband, steel-plated ambition, and dollar-stretching creativity. In fact, the life of a visual effects family is anything but safe and secure. Marion works as a freelancer, a very in-demand freelancer, thankfully, but jobs go for months at a time, not years, and in early March 2014, we needed to rethink a few things. My racing schedule was one of them. Unfortunately, that meant I would not be running the Whidbey Island Marathon in Washington in mid-April, which was a bummer because I was looking forward to visiting with my stepbrother Jeff and his adorable gaggle of little girls. Another time, for sure. Instead, what I needed to find was a race within driving distance, instead of flying distance. Thankfully, I did not need to search for long until I found the perfect "hometown" race that would offer up a whole new kind of challenge: racing two marathons within three weeks.

Oh, and one more thing, this one was a trail marathon, *yee-haw*! Yep, marathon thirty-three would be the Griffith Park Trail Marathon on Saturday, March 29.

I was not too nervous about the trail aspect of this race because I had already conquered the North Face Trail Marathon in the Marin Headlands back in December, and that course was an annihilator of the soul. If I could survive that race, I had faith I could survive any other trail race for the rest of my running days. However, my legs would not be fully recovered from the L.A. Marathon, which I had run three weeks prior in early March. But I wanted to run it, it fit the bill (literally), and once again I was excited to run around and above my gorgeous Los Angeles, this time on comfy, cushy dirt.

When race morning came around, I was excited, and relieved not to have to worry about a specific time to hit. Because trail runs generally take much longer than a road race, I could relax and just let myself enjoy the day and see where I shook out. The starting line was buzzing in the dark pre-dawn hours with a breed of runner that is more jovial then most and little nuttier too: the ultra-runner. This was not an ultra-marathon—actually the course did go a little over 26.2 miles although it was still advertised as a marathon—but that did not stop the ultra-runners from coming. They were there among us mortals, and I felt honored to feel like an amateur in their presence. I was eavesdropping on stories that made me weep with admiration; it was a sign that this was going to be a brilliant day.

The first seven miles were tough. There were lots of up,

up, down, and down-even- steeper around twisty bends of loose sandy dirt native to the chaparral landscape within Griffith Park. I knew I was keeping a decent pace, even though I didn't pay attention to my watch. I felt good, and was hanging with a few shaggy lookin' yet swift-footed dudes, so I knew I was doing all right. We hit a long ten-mile stretch of virtually flat land as we wound our way around the park and the Los Angeles Zoo, which was fine, but I wish I would have researched the course better. I would have picked up my pace along that stretch, but instead, I just continued running a mellow, controlled pace, anxious about the looming hills ahead.

Luckily, my intuition was correct about needing to conserve energy, because the last seven miles of the course tossed us into the hills again, and wow, that was a treat. It was much more up and up, then down. I think mile 18 was the first time in my running life when I felt truly pressed up against the mat, suffocating and taunted to tap out by nature. I was on a sheer single track trail on the back-side section of the park. I knew other runners were around me somewhere but I felt alone, and needed to punch this course in the mouth, so I just cranked slowly up that hill, crested the top, opened up my stride and giggled on my way down the other side. Silly trails, you can't break this nutcase of a runner.

I was spit back into civilization abruptly around mile twenty-one when I took a right turn down the fire road and was among other runners, day hikers, and horses. Sweet. This was a very exposed part of the course, and the day was heating up. I had my hydration pack on, so I was okay water-wise, but I knew I needed to finish soon and take a nice long swig of electrolyte- infused sports drink, so my focus shifted from "Running on trails is so fun and pretty," to "get to the finish line, ASAP."

The next five miles or so were a mix of cheers with fellow runners, and dodging big and small off-leash dogs as well as annoyed families being dragged out to nature to spend time together instead of passing mind-numbing hours on the couch. Ah, Los Angeles. I felt inspired by my fellow Angelenos' zest for the outdoors, but there were no barriers keeping these crowds from the course like there had been on Hollywood Boulevard just a few weeks before at the L.A. Marathon. Today I needed to "share the trail," so I leaped and darted around every civilian as safely as possible and ran down the hill to the finish as fast as I could.

I was alone for the last mile or so into the finish chute. There were slight cheers and enthusiasm from the crowd, but it was by far the most low-key finish line I had ever run across. I appreciated its understated integrity. As I was picking up my finisher's belt buckle, the race director came up to me and thanked me for bringing my hydration backpack. Suddenly I felt like I was part of the Trail Runners gang. I was no longer just a spoiled road runner whining about the flavor of the free sports drink handed out at the aid stations, but a *real* runner ready for anything the trails and that saucy minx Mother Nature threw at me. Plus, did I mention I earned a belt buckle?

I felt like I matured a lot during that race because I had planned around a "life hiccup" and had still finished marathon #33 on schedule, in fact ahead of schedule. I placed

7th overall female and 2nd in my age group in 4:31. Not too shabby, considering I had run a marathon less than a month earlier. Plus, I fell in love with trails that day, even though I am not built for them (my legs are too long). I knew trail races would play a big role in my running future. In essence, the Griffith Park Trail Marathon was a fun and challenging romp among friends and inner demons, my favorite kind of race.

Taryn Spates

Marathon #34 – The Mountains To the Sea Marathon, 2014

Channeling Iris McKay

I have always had tremendous respect and admiration for elite runners who are able to consistently run ninety-plus mile weeks in their training leading up to races. I have typically kept my weekly averages in the mid-fifty-mile range, because I need to fit in time to swim and ride my bike, and those activities eat up a lot of precious daylight. However, after I finished my "March Madness" month of two marathons, I decided that I wanted to put the bike and swim training on the back burner. I had to amp up my run training in preparation for my "A" race of the year: the Mountains to the Beach Marathon taking place on May 25 in Ventura, California. This race was high on my priority list because I knew it would be fast. It was literally all downhill, starting in Ojai and ending 26.2 miles down the road in Ventura. Yes, that Ojai. It was Iris McKay's favorite place on earth, and she would always try to drag Dylan off to Ojai in the high school years of *Beverly Hills 90210*. Iris was right: Ojai is lovely. I knew I could train specifically for this race; it had my undivided attention. I was

191

excited to test myself with the kind of training I had always wanted to try, but had been too scared to attempt. This was my chance.

My friend and coach Hadara was on board with my challenge and laid out some spectacular workouts for me over the six-week ramp up to the race after my Griffith Park finish. I did add on a few miles here and there to reach the weekly numbers I wanted, which she was okay with, but I pretty much stuck to her plan: week one, start with sixty miles, then increase every week until I tapped out at ninety miles per week. For the last eighteen months or so I had been faithful to the sixteen-mile long run, no more, no less; a trick I pulled out of Hanson's Running Project. But this time around I needed to load up a few more miles to my long run: seventeen, eighteen, nineteen, and twenty, here I come! However, the key to my big jump was having at least two workouts per day: a longer one in the morning, and a recovery jaunt in the afternoon/early evening. In my experience, this is a somewhat civilized way to crush yourself, long/hard running in the morning, short/mellow running in the afternoon. I have tried the opposite, short then long, and it is just a brutal way to live your life. That said, what is the secret magic trick of it all? That's simple: eating properly and having plenty of nutrition before, during and after runs.

I could go into how each day felt, each run in fact, but I will sum up by saying that when I reached my weekly mileage goals, I felt like I had just aced a final exam, because I needed to be calculated, consistent and resilient day after exhausting day. This kind of training was numbing and exhilarating. I was excited and nervous every day when I woke up and assessed my day ahead. I treated it like a job, which has kind of been the case for my Ironman training for years, but this race prep was me living an "out of reach" lifestyle that I never dreamed I could handle. Even though it was not pretty at times, I never cried, but I almost passed out on more than a few occasions. Still, I reached my ninety-mile weekly goal at the end of it all, and knew that I was more prepared for this marathon than any other. Number thirty-four was going to be legendary.

I drove up to Ventura the night before the race because I had to catch a very early bus to Ojai on race morning. Also, I felt like I earned this treat after putting forth the most brutal training block to date. So, Saturday afternoon, I was out my door and off I went seventy-five minutes up the coast to sleepy, yummy Ventura. I spent a few hours walking the small town. The surfer vibe made me feel right at home. Later I gobbled up a tasty pancake dinner, and actually caught a few peaceful zzzs before the 4 a.m. wake-up call.

As I exited my hotel in the dewy ocean air, I made some quick friends out of fellow runners walking to the bus stop. They were from Chicago, and laid out the quick times they wanted to hit during our pre-dawn chit-chat session, so I knew this race would live up to the hype as a near-shoe-in Boston qualifier. I was excited about the heavy downhill. Even with my disastrous past with heavy downhill marathons like Tucson, I felt good about this one. I had faith that my thunderous "cycling" quads could handle the constant pounding of my 150-pound bod against the pavement for over three hours. It might get ugly, but I was up for it.

The race start was a bit odd because there were port-o-lets lined up along the streets for blocks, but the lines moved at glacial pace. I decided comfort was more important than starting position, and put all my trust into my timing chip. Due to my back-of-the-pack starting position, I was motivated to bounce and dart my way through the very speedy field. Once we hit the bike path, a bottleneck would be unavoidable, so this big girl ran as fast as she could to find the perfect pace-mates once the course got real.

An odd feeling washed over me at about the ten-mile mark. It was as if my mind was not quite in rhythm with my legs, and I started to feel light-headed, and unknowingly slowed my pace. I knew I needed fuel, so I popped an energy chew and told my legs to keep going. This fast pace was exactly what we had been training for. Now was the time to go for it! Sub 3:20 baby!!!

Farther down the hill, I tasted salt in the air and knew the ocean was close, but I still had the last annoying seven miles to slog through before I would be done for the day. Suddenly, my GPS lost its connection to the satellite. Mile seventeen lasted *waaay* too long, which meant I was on my own for pacing... hmm. It was a good thing this was not my first rodeo. It was time to dust off my "perceived effort" skills and take it home to the finish.

The last two miles were grinding. I felt like a slug, but then I saw the finish-line banner about 600 meters down the beach and I decided to switch on my "Vista" speed and obliterate myself in an effort to creep under 3:20. I picked off a few runners in the chute. One girl seemed a little annoyed, but I'm sure she learned a lesson that day: give the finish *everything* you have, and don't be afraid to shatter your competitors' dreams. It's a race.

Once I crossed the line I looked at my watch: 3:20:26. So close…. I stumbled around my super-fast comrades reaching for water bottles, then plopped down on the grass and smiled. I only had one more marathon before this quest would be complete. Next up was marathon thirty-five.

Taryn Spates

Marathon #35 – The San Francisco Marathon, 2014

A Big Slice of Humble Pie

There is something both sensational and horrific about accomplishing a goal. I set a goal I knew was within my grasp, but far enough ahead of me that I did not have to worry about reaching it and moving beyond it for a couple of years. Then suddenly, those years were up.

I finished my thirty-fifth marathon on July 27, 2014. I can't believe it happened, but I know it did because I was there. I was grossly appreciative of how painful an experience it was from before the start to after the finish. Actually, that may be a bit dramatic, but it was a difficult experience. I can still taste every mile. I wasn't myself that day. Or maybe I was actually my true self, stripped of the fast running façade that had fleeced my persona the last eighteen months. I do know that I was not who I wanted to be. I felt bad, I ran slow, I was passed by thousands of runners, yet for some sick reason I am happy it went down the way it did. I needed to be humbled.

I flew up to Oakland on Saturday morning; I took the BART for the first time over to the city, and chatted it up with a mother/daughter SoCal half-marathon running duo who were in town to run the race. I did not mention the marathon would be my thirty-fifth, and as such the culmination of a two-and-a-half-year quest of self-preservation and motivation. However, I did share that I was running the marathon. I was excited about the course this time around because we would be running over the Golden Gate Bridge, a new addition since my first stint in 2003, and a real treat for any native Californian, or citizen of the world for that matter.

I exited at the Embarcadero stop, grabbed some fuel from Noah's Bagels and started my walk down to the race expo being held at Fort Mason, where I would meet up with my sister Sarah who was running the race, too. Sarah mentioned that it was a pretty long walk, and that I should probably take a cab, but I wanted to stretch my legs and enjoy my mini-vacay weekend, so I said I would be fine. Cut to twenty minutes later: I flagged down a pedi-cab (the bicycle cabbies) and sat back to enjoy the ride to Fort Mason as a true tourist.

The expo was an absolute madhouse, but I met up with Sarah just fine, and met her friend Erin, who was an ambassador for the race, as well as a runner. Sarah and I sauntered back to her car along the strand next to Crissy Field. In fact, it was a preview of a section of the race course we would be running the next day. I savored this time with Sarah; it was wonderful to share this momentous milestone in my life with her. We have been on many adventures together over the years. For example, we explored Washington, DC all by ourselves one summer day when we were teenagers. We must have sat on fifteen park benches that day, solving all of the world's problems and riffing about our futures. We didn't always get along, especially when we were younger. She worshipped Mary and thought I was a tool, but we have grown closer every year, and I was so honored and relieved that she would be running my thirty-fifth marathon with me.

We chilled at her house for a few hours, doing the glamorous runner tasks such as foam rolling (or softball rolling in my case) while drinking water and prepping for a pre-race feast. Next, Sarah's friends Erin and Erin came over. One was the previously mentioned race ambassador, and the other was a carbon copy of Annie, one of my best friends from college. It was fun and refreshing to be spending quality time with such amazing women. A rare and real treat for me. We made pancakes and pasta, and shared running and life stories and goals for the race. I have to admit that my goals were not very ambitious. I was not feeling in top form after the previous four weeks (which included Ragnar and the June Lake Half-Ironman), but I felt that competitive burn to aim for at least 3:30. Ambassador Erin treated us to a white bracelet which gave us access to the Ambassador tent, which was exactly the VIP treatment I was looking for the finale of my quest. I did not expect it, but certainly did not it turn down. We all said our goodbyes and good lucks, and then the Erins were off in an Uber out into the San Francisco night.

The Kelly/Fox sisters were in bed by about 8. I think I was asleep by 9:30, and then we were up and at 'em by 3 a.m. I was aware of my body, and it did not feel as light and peppy as usual. However, I was excited to be sharing this wonderful experience with Sarah, I had a feeling she would be running a very special race. We headed toward the aforementioned Ambassador's tent where we chatted and chilled with the Erins and other happy runners underneath the illuminated Bay Bridge. The bridge's lights were still on, because the sun was not up. Yep, another 5:30 a.m. start time. *Bring it!*

We started in different waves. I was about two minutes ahead of the girls, but when the gun went off, so did my expectations for the day. I did not feel good. I was moving at my usual early miles sub-7:30 minute mile pace, but I just felt out of sync, tired and annoyed that there were no clear mile markers set up. Grr. Yes, I have a Garmin, but I still prefer a large sign letting me know I am making progress. The first few miles were littered with short, steep hills. I trudged up them confidently, but everyone else must have felt better about themselves because runners were flying by me in droves. I felt like I was stuck in second gear while they were flying up to fifth. When I finally let myself look at my watch, it read five miles. That was a shock. Those first five miles had flown by. *Whew!* Maybe I was not as far off my usual self as I had thought.

The next four to five miles took us over the Golden Gate Bridge, which was everything I hoped it would be. I finally felt strong, and found my groove, then I saw Sarah and "Annie" Erin on my way back over to the city. They both looked awesome, calm, cool and collected. Luckily, I still felt good at that point, so I probably looked good to them, too. But then we climbed a big hill leading into Golden Gate Park over mile ten and flew down a long, steep downhill on the other side. I love downhills, but once we hit the flats again around mile eleven, everything changed. I was thrilled to see Ambassador Erin fly past me up a neighborhood hill. For about three seconds, I thought I would catch up to her. Nope.

The next two-and-a-half hours were filled with slow running, measly expectations and overflowing gratitude. I never allowed myself to be sad and disappointed at how my body had finally tapped out. I *should* be spent. On my *best* day, on *anyone's* best day, marathons are hard. This race should be hard, that day and every other day. In shape or not, 26.2 miles is a long way to run, and I had been blessed to be running it for the thirty-fifth time. How could I be feeling anything but thankful at the many gifts this race had given me? I smiled and accepted that the marathon was teaching me a lesson, and feeding me humble pie instead of another gel. I needed it, and even wanted it. *The marathon saved me in every way a runner can be saved.* Please excuse the shameless *Titanic* reference; I couldn't help myself.

I experienced the best "pass" ever by a fellow runner around mile twenty-one. Sarah passed me looking great, and I waved her on with a pain-induced, proud smile. She was crushing it! I finally found my legs again around mile twenty-four, just enough time for me to enjoy the last two miles of this race, and the final leg of my quest to run thirty-five marathons by the time I turned thirty-five.

Once again, the San Francisco Marathon would prove to be a pivotal race in my journey. It had been eleven years before to the day when I first broke four hours and believed I could actually run marathons for real, and the Boston qualifier seed was planted. I am happy to report that I have run many fast marathons, and a few slow ones, and the secret is that they were all equally wonderful. A finish line is a finish line, no matter how long it takes to get there. Crossing over it never gets old.

Suffering near the finish

Taryn Spates

Marathon #36 – The Basel Marathon, 2014

One To Grow On

The culmination of my 35-by-35 quest was fitting, and respectful to the marathon and my love and passion for running. However, how it ended was not in my original plan. When I first started planning my fourteen races in earnest after my breakdown in Lake Cachuma, I remembered that there was a marathon in Basel, Switzerland right around my birthday in September. I had already researched the race because Tim had moved to Basel in 2010 with his family, and I had thought about sneaking in the marathon during a visit. Therefore, I thought running the Basel marathon as my thirty-fifth marathon would be a perfect way to end my quest.

Unfortunately, the date of the race kept slipping from one September weekend to the next, thwarting my delicate marathon schedule. Originally it was slated for September 7, then they moved it to the 28th, which was after my birthday — September 17 — so I figured, what was the point of that? I wanted to run "35 by 35," not "35 just after I turned 35." My mom thought it was no big deal, but I did. I had to finish the races before my birthday, so Basel suddenly did not fit in at all in the equation. Then my plans really flew off the rails when I decided on a whim while watching the Ironman World Championships on NBC that I would sign up for another Ironman, even though I had set a schedule for 2014 to be all about marathons. I decided to throw in all of my chips and go for it and sign up for Ironman Lake Tahoe. The race was scheduled for September 21. The flip side of that selfish decision was that Basel *really* would not be able to happen at all. I could not afford to race an Ironman (which are very expensive) and fly to Basel and run the marathon. Therefore, I decided to forgo Basel to focus on the Ironman and finish 35 by 35 before my birthday, thus throwing my original master plan out the window.

Cut to early May, when after enduring months of grueling training and soul-searching, I decided to truly take advantage of this moment in my life to test myself. I vowed to race Ironman Lake Tahoe on Sunday the 21st, rest for a couple of days, then fly to Switzerland and race the Basel marathon the following Sunday, the 28th. This ridiculous new proposition would take "going out with a bang" to a whole new level.

Along the way I had started to look for work, and then stopped to solely focus on my *big* races of the summer and the Ironman in September. But an opportunity came my way that I did not have the heart to say "no" to: Hannah's Varsity volleyball coach asked me to be the program coordinator for the Alemany Girls volleyball program, which was awesome. I had an inkling it would be a pretty demanding position and that my training might suffer, but I said "yes" because I wanted to help as much as possible and I wanted to be involved for Hannah's sake. Honestly, I don't think she really cared either way, but I took on the position. It was voluntary, of course, but wow, what a ton of work.

Miraculously, I was able to achieve all of the training for my races in May, June, and July, but the San Francisco Marathon humbled me. My body was finally yelping for some rest, when what I needed to do in my schedule was focus on six very intense weeks of Ironman training, which included an overwhelming emphasis on cycling due to the challenge of racing in Lake Tahoe. On top of that, this volleyball gig was shaping up to look more and more like a *real* job every day, mainly because I needed to be available at all times of the day for questions from parents and tasks from the coach. Even though I am confident that training for four to six hours per day would have been possible, it might have burdened the success of the program and the happiness of the players and parents. So, in early August I made the most excruciating decision I have in years—a decision that was almost as hard as when I decided not to play basketball my senior year of high school—I decided not to race Ironman Lake Tahoe.

Luckily, I was able to get back my money from the rental house in time, but was out more than $700 from the registration fee. Marion kept assuring me not to worry about it. I did have some cash from selling one of my bikes in July, which eased my conscience slightly. Next, I stopped my Ironman training and switched to recovery, and mainly running. No matter what I was going to run the Basel marathon on the 28th.

Let's fast forward to the morning of September 21 when I begrudgingly hopped online to Ironman.com to see what was happening at Ironman Lake Tahoe. "What the—?" The race had been canceled due to the heavy smoke from the Kings wildfire that had been surrounding the area. I felt terrible for all of the athletes who were at the starting line only to have their hopes dashed minutes before the gun went off. On the other hand—and I feel awful admitting this—I was relieved that I was actually not missing the race at all. I know that's horrible, but I am human. There have been many opinions bouncing around about how the WTC handled the call, but I have faith it was the right move. Safety first, my friends. Personally, I was thrilled to have that deadening weight lifted from my shoulders. Finally, I was able to fully enjoy my last few days before flying to Switzerland and could look forward to running the marathon with fresh legs, an open mind, and Grinch-like bursting heart. This was it.

A *huge* reason that I wanted to run the marathon in Basel was to share the experience with Tim (who, as I have mentioned earlier, was the original marathoner in my life), but also to create memories with my nieces Jenna and Kate, and nephew Blake. I want to fully embrace my role as "Adventurous Aunt T," and I figured running the marathon in their new city would solidify my street cred.

I had decided a while before that I did not want to have children of my own. It's a controversial and baffling choice to many, but it is the right one for me. In fact, one of the reasons I enjoyed my time in Basel so much was that both my brother Tim and his Super-Hero wife Shannon never asked me once about having kids. They asked about Hannah. I know my calling in life was to be her stepmother, and to inspire my many nieces and nephews to go after their dreams. Even if their parents think they are nutty, I will always be there in their corner, rooting them on.

A bonus part of the trip was that I had a sneak peek into my future while talking to twenty-five or so eager International School Basel students during their lunch hour the Friday before the race. Shannon had spoken about me with the school's PE teacher, a handsome and vibrant Frenchman named Didier, and he had jumped at the chance for me to share my experiences with the students. I was a little nervous, but I was more excited than anything, and was excited to share my experiences with running and triathlon with the next generation. The highlight of the day had to have been Blake standing next to me in front of his peers, giving me a fantastic introduction. I was both impressed and humbled; I didn't know he knew that much about me.

I started off talking about how long a marathon is, and what it takes to train for one, but I opened it up to questions pretty quickly because I knew the kids were there voluntarily because they were interested in running. They asked such inquisitive, excellent questions. Thankfully I had answers, maybe not the right ones, but I gave them all feedback, and hopefully some inspiration to start and keep running themselves. I also wanted them to know that they can run for the rest of their lives, not just when they are young. I shared with them that I could run a mile faster at thirty-five than I could at fifteen. I think that got them excited, especially the girls. Eventually, the kids had to go back to class, but not before a few of them, mainly the tall girls who reminded me so much of myself at that age, came up and asked me individual questions. They looked at me like I was their hero; it was the coolest feeling ever. Next, it was up to me to live up to their expectations and run fast on Sunday.

Fortunately, Saturday was an action-packed family day which included Blake's soccer game, a detour through France to visit a Swiss castle, a stop by the race expo, and an hour so in my mother's would-be "heaven" — the Kurbis Festival (that's Pumpkin Festival for us English-speaking folks). Sadly, I did not partake in the delicious Kurbis soup, due to my strict diet before race day. It would be another pancake dinner for me later, but Jenna and Shannon gobbled some up for all of us. Next, we conquered the corn maze under the steadfast leadership of Jenna. I would follow her into battle any day.

I slept well on Saturday night, but not a whole lot. I have grown accustomed to my usual 4 a.m. wake-up call on race days, but with the 8:30 a.m. start time, that early rising hour was not required. I was up and at 'em anyway. Tim and I left for the tram around 6:50 because I told him I wanted to be at the starting line an hour before the gun went off. However, we were both a little surprised when we arrived at our stop and nary a barricade was up yet, let alone crowds of runners in the street. We walked around for a little while, and he showed me his favorite spot overlooking the Rhine River, just behind a cathedral. We found a clutch breakfast spot for him to have coffee and a chocolate croissant, and a warm place for me to sit, just a block away from the starting line, and right in front of the finish line.

The runners started bustling about the starting line as Tim and I both assessed the crowd. He said I had a chance to do well, but I am always on the lookout for the spritely swift-footed 40-50-something runners who seem to edge me out of the top spot. I saw a couple of bogeys, so my expectations were not too high. I was just thrilled and thankful to be there, yet again standing on another marathon starting line, feeling fresh and pumped to give everything I had for another 26.2 miles (er, 42.2 kilometers, for you European folks out there).

The gun went off and I started off quickly but maintained a sensible position considering the narrow cobblestone streets. The most annoying/hilarious few hundred yards of the race happened when I got stuck behind two pace runners, being slapped and punched by the balloons tied on their shirts (*next time, carry signs, my friends*). However, just after the 2K mark, the kilometer markings became a fun change for me because they popped up a whole lot sooner than mile markers, of course, which kept me entertained and motivated throughout the race. I darted around my balloon-smacking cohorts at the corner just beyond the 2K mark, and settled into a comfortably uncomfortable pace that I felt confident in maintaining for most of the race. Honestly, it was fun to be running fast again.

The most amazing part of this marathon was that Tim was rooting for me in person. It could be because I am the youngest of us four Kelly kids, or just that I am just a big sap, but I have always had a soft spot when it comes to spending time with my siblings. My favorite place in the world was sitting in the back seat of Tim's beat-up Honda Accord, driving to and from our parents' houses in the late '80s and early '90s. During those precious hours I felt protected and insulated from the world because all four of us were together. There is no doubt that I adored Tim, Peter and Mary growing up, but when Tim went away to college I was only ten, and it was not an easy transition for me. Tim was a rock for the three of us elementary-aged kiddos when we moved from Palos Verdes to Claremont after our parents' divorce. His approval meant everything to me, because he was the man of the house, and that feeling has not changed over the last thirty years. I believed running this marathon in Basel with Tim cheering me on meant just as much to my thirty-five-year-old self as it did to my ten-year-old self: absolutely everything.

I wasn't sure when or where I would see him on the course, but it didn't matter, because he was everywhere! The first spot was just after the 10K mark, which was perfect because he let me know I was the second woman. Sweet! Just after I saw him I noticed my shoes were untied, so I had to stop and tie them. I think I only lost a few seconds, but really? Shoes untied, come on Taryn! Over the next few miles, we meandered through some tree-lined old roads within Basel. There were some ups and downs in elevation that altered my pace a bit, but I felt strong and consistent throughout the first of two loops on the course. Then I saw Tim again and he yelled,

"How are you?"

"Okay, I'm kind of feeling it."

"Just have fun, Tar. The leader is 200 feet in front of you!"

Well, that did the trick! The slight twinge of lactic acid

built up in my legs went away as suddenly I felt like a real competitor.

I had never been this close to the lead in any marathon or triathlon. In fact, the only time I won races was in the 100-meter hurdles in high school, and those were mainly in the preliminary heats. I did lead a cross-country race for the first mile during my fleet-footed freshman season. It was the Frosh/Soph heat at the Mt. Sac Relays. The first mile on the Mt. Sac course is flat, then a little windy. I clocked it in 6:34 minutes, my fastest time to date, but I fell back a few places once we hit the unforgiving switchbacks. Then I fell further back once I started the climb up Poop Out hill—sadly no podium finish on that day. However, the feeling of being out in front, with every other runner outside of your periphery and behind you is a feeling an athlete never forgets.

As I rounded the next turn in the Basel race, I saw a petite blonde woman in a triathlon kit about fifty feet ahead of me. I assumed she was the leader. My pace was faster, so I didn't make a heroic surge or anything; soon enough I overtook her and ran ahead. We gave each other a courteous nod, but she didn't try to chase me down. That was it. A few yards ahead I saw a guy on a bike riding in the middle of the street, with a sign on the front. I assumed he was the first place female escort, so I asked him, "Am I in first place?" He turned to me, looking somewhat bewildered to see another woman who was nearly double the size of the pipsqueak he was riding next to for the first 21K,

"Marathon?"

"Yes."

"Yeah."

That was all I needed to hear. My life was complete. I was leading a marathon. What??!!

The next 21K was spectacular. There were out-and-back sections of the course where we ran past fellow marathoners and half-marathoners, and one thing I always do is cheer for the lead women in races when I see them. I believe the race is against ourselves, not each other, and I revere fast runners, so it was pretty surreal that I was the one these runners were cheering for.

Yes, my legs started to ache over the last 10K or so, but I kept a consistent pace. In fact, I passed quite a few prideful Basler men who were not too keen on a woman overtaking them, but this was my day. I was a machine. This was my thirty-sixth marathon, for goodness' sake. I knew what I was doing, and all I wanted to say was, "On your left, thanks."

The last kilometer or so seemed to go on forever, but soon enough I made the final turn and ran up toward the finish. I was looking for Tim in the crowds lining both sides of the street, but I was ecstatic when I saw Shannon, Jenna, Kate, and Tim cheering for me and holding the cutest sign ever just before I made the final turn toward the finish line. I didn't think the girls would be able to make it to the race because they were in various states of illness, but Shannon rallied the troops, and I will be forever grateful that the girls were able to see their Aunt T win a marathon. This trip was about creating memories with them, and I think they will remember that for a long time. What a way to end my 35-by-35 journey: winning my thirty-sixth marathon in Basel, Switzerland in front of Tim and his family. I couldn't have made up a better ending.

Leading the Basel Marathon

Epilogue

What I've Been Up To

I have kept myself fairly busy this last year since completing 35-by-35. I ran Boston again—this time it was freezing, especially for this weak SoCal girl, but it was amazing. I ran it fast this time. I finished in 3:25, nearly fifty minutes faster than the first time I ran it ten years prior at age twenty-five. I also wrote this book. I discovered that I am a writer above all else, but like running, there is always room for improvement.

The most important lesson I learned was that even though this particular quest is complete, there will be many more for me, and I hope there will many more for all of you, too. I will keep racing marathons and triathlons all over the world and writing about them for at least another thirty-five years. I promise.

It doesn't have to be running marathons, or running at all. We are all capable of amazing things if we set a goal and challenge ourselves to go after it.

Taryn Spates

Acknowledgements

I would like to acknowledge the following fabulous people for helping me throughout my 35 by 35 journey. First off, my husband Marion, who has been a steadfast cheerleader in every challenge I have taken on over the last eleven years. My step-daughter, Hannah, who is growing up to be a striking and capable human being. My mom, Madelynn Miller, who has always been in my corner as a writer, and athlete. My dad, Peter Kelly, my newest writing fan, and number one Ironman spectator. My siblings, Tim, Peter, Mary, Chris, Jen, Sarah, Bo, Kendra and Jeff, you all have made me who I am today, thank you. To their equally, if not more so amazing significant others, Shannon, Alexa, Jim, Debbie, Curt, Eric, Carly, Konstantin and Amy, thank you for loving my favorite people. To my step-parents, Kent Miller and Sally Kelly, thank you for loving not only my mom and dad, but all of us kiddos, too. I am blessed to have the support of my mother in-law, Muriel Spates.

To all of my amazing girlfriends, Emily, Hadara, Hillary, Annie, Sarah, Susie and Chanda, thank you for making me laugh. I want to give a special thanks to my god mother Julie Hill and long-time family friend Dianne Johnson who have given me unique perspectives on how to tell my story. Thank you to my early readers, Jenny Fengler, Mary Skerrett Koff, and Sarah Fox, you helped mold my story into a book. Also, thank you to my proofreader Susan Fish, you made me look good! Thank you to my Aunt Corrie, Uncle Fred, Uncle Len, Aunt Susan, Uncle Pat, Aunt Lynn, Uncle Tad, and Aunt Jan who have been my super-fans all my life. Thank you to my amazing cousins, Erin, Patrick, Beth and Megan, you all are equally beautiful and hilarious people I wish I could visit with more often. Many hugs go out to my nieces and nephews who I hope will join me on many adventures in the future, Dylan, Sean, Nick, Blake, Jenna, Kate, Sidney, Kaia, Reed, Tristan, Thalia, Lyla, Cassie, and Darby. And, most importantly thank you to my grandmother, Dorothy Norris. My grandmother told me to "keep writing" every time I visited with her until her passing at a mighty 94 years young.

Last, but certainly not least, thank you my dear readers. I am thrilled that you read my story, and I would love to hear from you! I can be reached through my website: www.tarynspates.com.

My grandmother, Dorothy Norris

About the Author

Taryn is a writer and runner who lives for storytelling and adventure. She is a daughter, sister, wife, stepmother and California native currently living in the majestic San Fernando Valley.

Taryn graduated with a Bachelor of Arts degree in Film Studies from the University of Colorado at Boulder, then went on to pursue a career in Visual Effects in film and television production.

Taryn wrote her first book after being inspired to run thirty-five marathons by the time she turned thirty-five years old.

Made in the USA
San Bernardino, CA
14 April 2017